Patricia Wilson-Kastner

THE PREACHER AS JACOB

THE PREACHER AS JACOB

A New Paradigm for Preaching

Kenneth L. Gibble

THE SEABURY PRESS

All biblical references are to the Revised Standard Version of the
Bible: Old Testament Section, copyright © 1952; New Testament
Section First Edition, copyright © 1946; Second Edition © 1971
by Division of Christian Education of the National Council of
Churches of Christ in the United States of America.

Grateful acknowledgment is made for the following:

From Abingdon Press, permission to quote from the
Interpreter's Dictionary Of The Bible. Copyright © 1962.

From Princeton University Press, permission to quote from
The Collected Works of C. G. Jung, trans. R. F. C. Hull,
Bolingen Series 20, Vol. II: *Psychology and Religion: West and East.*
Copyright © 1958.

From Schocken Books, Inc., permission to quote from
Godwrestling by Arthur I. Waskow. Copyright © 1978.

Cover design: Art Direction, Inc.
Copyright © 1985 by Kenneth L. Gibble

Library of Congress Catalog Card Number: 83-16501
ISBN: 0-86683-985-2

Printed in the United States of America.
5   4   3   2   1

Winston Press
430 Oak Grove
Minneapolis, Minnesota 55403

to Jim, who pushes

Acknowledgments

My thanks to Dr. Lauree Hersch Meyer and Dr. James Poling, both faculty members of Bethany Theological Seminary, Oak Brook, Illinois, for their encouragement of this project. Rooted more deeply in the past is the debt I owe to the preachers whose words awoke me as a child to the power of the proclaimed word: Allen Becker, Rufus Bucher, Henry Hess, Howard A. Merkey, and Wilmer A. Petry, to name but a few. Earle W. Fike, Jr., my preaching mentor, confirmed in me the hunch that finding the right words mattered. Finally, I acknowledge with gratitude the contribution of members of the Ridgeway Community Church of the Brethren, my indispensable partners in preaching for fourteen years.

CONTENTS

INTRODUCTION

There are times when a fortuitous (providential?) reading of the right book can have profound consequences. In this case, the book was Rollo May's *Love and Will*; I was re-reading it after ten years.

> The daimonic is the urge in every being to affirm itself, assert itself, perpetuate and increase itself.... We can repress the daimonic, but we cannot avoid the toll of apathy and the tendency toward later explosion which such repression brings in its wake.[1]

It was this reference to the "daimonic" that helped me bring together a number of personal and professional experiences with a name that fit. As I reflected further, I began to see that the idea of the daimonic had vast implications, not only for my personal experience, but for my ministry as well. This book has grown out of my efforts to explore the meaning of the daimonic and, in turn, to assess that meaning in terms of its impact on Christian preaching.

A word is in order about the "personal and professional experiences" mentioned above. I was reared in a home and church setting where the outward expression of feelings was discouraged. In such a situation, one learns to control one's feelings. The psychological term is *repression*. In other words, if I want to be spared the pain of continually keeping my feelings in check, I will be likely not to allow those feelings into conscious awareness. That way, I can more easily suppose they do not really exist. This is especially true of anger, fear, grief, and other parts of human experience often assigned negative value. But there is a price to pay for repression. In the words of the poet, "If my devils leave me, I am afraid my angels will take flight as well."[2]

The alternative to repression is set forth by May.

> You take in the daimonic which would possess you if you didn't. The one way to get over daimonic possession is to process it by frankly confronting it, coming to terms with it, integrating it into the self-system.[3]

As these quotations make clear, denial of the "devils" inevitably leads to denial of the "angels." This discovery came to me recently when I heard someone describe a dream in which he was approached by a wolf. He was frightened by the wolf until he realized that it was part of himself, his own dark, potentially evil side. Only when he reached out to make friends with the wolf was he able to move towards health and self-acceptance.

Madeleine L'Engle says it this way:

> Righteousness begins to reveal itself as that strength which is so secure that it can show itself as gentleness, and the only people who have this kind of righteousness are those who are integrated and do not suppress the dark side of themselves.[4]

For myself, and I believe for most ministers, the "dark side" of ourselves is precisely what is suppressed—and for good reasons. Some ministers (as I did) will discover the dark side in their repressed feelings. Others will find it in the untapped rational, sensate, or intuitive parts of their psyches. But whichever of these elements represents the "dark side," we keep it under wraps. Why? Because we learned early that virtue was rewarded, by approval, by attention, by being told how "good" we were. What better way to be good than to identify ourselves with the moral guardian of society, the church? Here, more than anywhere else, goodness is expected and rewarded. All of which means that the very possibility of its opposite must be denied.

In dreams, however, the "wolf" in us will emerge. Becoming conscious of my own dreams was a great help in beginning to get in touch with the dark side of myself and to embrace it, accept it as part of *me*. It is, I discover, the source of great power, this daimonic. When, instead of turning from it in fear, I turn towards it in loving, yet respectful affirmation, I find it enabling me to draw on the creative gifts I have. I find it helping me to reach out with my whole self to others in the intimacy of friendship and pastoral care. I find myself able to tell others I love them, or, if appropriate, to tell them they arouse in me rage or bewilderment or fear. I find myself marveling at what happens when my struggle with the biblical text releases the power to create a sermon, to write and speak words that become a means of grace to the people of the congregation.

All this is confessional and thus necessarily subjective. In order to make this inward dynamic understandable, I shall first of all give attention to the historical roots of the concept of the daimonic. I will then explore the writings of a psychologist, C. G. Jung, a theologian, Paul Tillich, and a literary artist, Ursula LeGuin, as a means of summarizing some contemporary explications of the daimonic. The relationships between the daimonic and the preaching task are given detailed attention in Chapters III through V. I attempt to demonstrate there how the daimonic can become part of the interplay between biblical text, human experience, and the consequent preaching event. The final chapter offers a concrete example of this interplay through an exegesis and commentary on Gen. 32:22–32 and a drama/ sermon based on that text.

It is my contention that in recognizing the daimonic in ourselves, naming it, claiming it as part of our created selves, we who are called to ministry experience the releasing of a power that can, by the grace of God, create and heal. In the preaching event, that power, if released, becomes a dynamic which comforts, judges, or inspires preacher and hearer alike. A living word is turned loose.

Nevertheless, encountering the daimonic in preaching, as in every other instance, is a risky venture. Like the patriarch Jacob, we may very well come out of the fray wounded, maimed. Rollo May, commenting on the task of the literary artist, says that the writer's motive is to find a solution to a problem. The solution consists of a wider and deeper dimension of conscious-ness *"to which the writer is carried by virtue of his wrestling with the problem."*[5] How much more is this true for the preacher! *Wrestling* is indeed the proper word to describe the preacher's personal, existential encounter with the biblical text. Any-thing less is a failure to take seriously the preaching vocation. But the preacher wrestles also with his or her own humanity. And the preacher tries to see in the lives of parishioners, lives often filled with pain and anxiety, the hand of God. Indeed, in encountering the daimonic, whether in the intrapersonal or the interpersonal arena, we find the hands of God grasping us, contending with us. And yet it is a grappling for our own and our people's good. We are wounded, but we prevail. And from the experience may flow the creating, healing, enlivening power of God.

CHAPTER I

HISTORICAL SURVEY
OF THE DAIMONIC

Daimons and Demons in the Old Testament

It is necessary, at the outset, to distinguish between two words: *daimon* and *demon*. The former, a Greek spelling, contains within its definition the possibility for either good or evil. As used by ancient writers, the daimonic referred to an anonymous god or a personification of vague, mysterious powers believed to operate alongside major deities and to affect both natural and human events.[1] *Demon*, on the other hand, is a more modern word which denotes a malign spirit or devil. In this study the Greek spelling will be used most often because its connotations are more consonant with the ideas and themes to be explored. The words *demon* and *demonic* in this chapter will be reserved for reference to specifically evil figures or forces.

In his informative discussion of the biblical understanding of the daimonic, T. H. Gaster notes that the Hebrew word *elohim* is often used in the Old Testament to mean much the same as what the ancient Greeks meant when they spoke of someone receiving a flash of inspiration from a god, or daimon. He cites the example from Gen. 30:8 where Rachel declares, at the birth of Naphtali, that she has been wrestling with her sister Leah "with the wrestlings of elohim." Says Gaster: "what she means is that she has been struggling with her as if possessed by a daimon."[2]

Disease and other causes of death are often personified in Old Testament writings. For example, Ps. 91:5–6: "You will not fear the terror of the night . . . nor the pestilence that stalks at darkness, nor the destruction that wastes at noonday." Gaster sees in these personifications a specific reference to a demon "analogous to the Akkadian *muttalik mūsí*, 'night-stalker.' "[3] Whether or not such personifications are attributable to specific demons of Israel's neighbors, it is clear that the Hebrews attributed human difficulties to outside forces acting upon them.

Henry Kelly claims for the Old Testament writers a superiority in these matters. He states that in almost all primitive cultures one finds an abundance of *demons*, "malevolent invisible beings" responsible for various human ills and tribulations. "It is therefore an indication of the sophistication of the Hebrew religion in its official form that very little of this perspective is evident in the writings of the Old Testament."[4] Kelly admits that references to demonic beings from surrounding cultures do appear in the Old Testament, but he argues that these seem to reflect only a kind of literary decoration.

Despite Kelly's praise for the "sophistication" of the Old Testament, the evidence suggests that references to demons known by Israel's neighbors were an attempt to deal with them directly, rather than to employ them merely for literary purposes. For example, in Deut. 32:17, which refers to sacrificing to "demons," and in Lev. 17:7, which mentions sacrifices to "satyrs," both terms denote objects of pagan worship. In these and similar cases, it is stated that some Israelites were guilty of engaging in sacrifices to them.

Several specific demons are mentioned in the Old Testament. Lilith, a Babylonian female demon, alluded to in Isa. 34:14, appears in Mesopotamian texts as a succubus who visited men at night.[5] Resheph, the Canaanite god of plague and pestilence, is mentioned in Deut. 32:24 as a punishment God will bring upon the people.[6] References to these and other demons may have been used only as figures of speech. Scholars are divided on this issue. Gaster's statement regarding the place of the daimonic in biblical writings is pertinent enough to this study to merit an extended quotation.

> With the development of monotheism — i.e., when the idea of a single cosmic deity supersedes that of a congress of controlling powers — daimons and spirits tend to become subordinated to that central figure and regarded as his ministers or "angels" (envoys); or else they coalesce into a single "holy spirit" which emanates from him, represents the totality of his ergative powers, and serves to diffuse his personality throughout the world of his creation.
>
> From the standpoint of religious psychology, daimonism represents an externalization of human experiences. Feelings and sensations, moods and impulses, even physical conditions, which might otherwise be described as obtaining autonomously *within* a man, are portrayed, on this basis, as outer forces working *upon* him. Aspiration becomes inspiration; ecstasy, rapture (i.e., a state of being "seized"); insight, revelation. Emotion becomes, so to speak, *im*motion; that which is *pro*jected out of the self, that which is *in*jected into it; the flight of imagination, a flight inward, not outward, an invasion rather than an escape. In the language of daimonism, therefore, all such experiences are represented as visitations — i.e., as actions of an external power, rather than as internal psychic states.[7]

Of special interest in the study of the daimonic in the Old Testament is the emergence of Satan. Nowhere in the Old Testament is Satan said to be a distinctive demonic personage, in enmity with God and the source of all evil. The word *satan*, as it appears in the book of Job, is a common noun, having the fundamental meaning of adversary. When the word is used in 1 Chron. 21:1, *satan*, or a *satan* is said to have incited David

to take a census. It is not possible to determine whether the
satan is considered evil here; in 2 Sam. 24:1, it is God who
persuades David to take the census. However, in light of the
2 Samuel narrative's claim that God does so because he is angry
with David, it can be inferred that a negative connotation is
associated with the satan. Furthermore, in the book of Job the
satan is portrayed as cynical, skeptical of human virtue, and
not very ethical in his efforts to expose what he regards as Job's
questionable righteousness.[8]

Demons in Later Jewish Writings and the New Testament

Scholars are in general agreement that Jewish thought regarding demons during the intertestamental period was greatly
influenced by Mesopotamian demonology. As a result, the
daimons or anonymous gods were now considered to be devils
or evil spirits. These malevolent beings, as described in apocry-
phal and pseudepigraphal literature, had the power to inflict
misfortune and disaster on the world and also to tempt men
and women into evil ways. The demons are frequently referred to as unclean spirits whose task is destruction. Thus in Jub.
10:5, the "spirits" are described as "malignant, and created in
order to destroy."

In popular Judaism the demons were subject to their master,
usually named Belial or Satan or Mastemah. The demons, it
was thought, would lose their power in the messianic age.
"Then shall all the spirits of deceit be given to be trodden
under foot, and men shall rule over wicked spirits" (Testament
of Simeon 6:6). The destiny of the demons is everlasting punishment. "And there shall be no spirit of deceit of Beliar, For
he shall be cast into the fire forever" (Testament of Judah
25:3).

The postexilic emphasis on demons posed problems for the
orthodox position, which feared a challenge to the monotheistic supremacy of Yahweh. Gaster states that orthodoxy felt

impelled to offer an alternative explanation for the evil which befell humanity. It did so, first, by substituting for the hosts of demons a special order of destructive forces commissioned by Yahweh to wreak destruction on the ungodly. In Ecclus. 39:28–31, these forces are identified with natural phenomena, wind, fire, and hail, and are said to be "created for vengeance." A second alternative turned the demons into fallen angels, subjects of Yahweh who had rebelled against him, descended to earth, and perverted humanity. In the Old Testament, Gen. 6:1–4 gives an example of this belief; the story is expanded in Jub. 5:1–3. The apostate angels, or *Watchers*, as they are called in the Pseudepigrapha, were disqualified from reentry into heaven and would eventually be destroyed by fire.[9]

Thus, despite the influence of dualistic thought which the popular notion of demons brought into Judaism, the essential oneness of God was maintained. "What is of theological importance is . . . that Jewish monotheism avoided an absolute dualism. . . . As far back as our knowledge goes of the history of evil angels and demons, God is always thought of as the creator of all spirits."[10]

In the New Testament, the existence of demons, as evil spirits responsible for many ills, is taken for granted. In Matt. 25:41, the demons are called the angels of Satan for whom eternal fire is prepared. All demons are under the command of the prince of demons who is called variously Satan, Belial, or Beelzebul. In addition to tempting persons to evil, Satan directs the demons or unclean spirits in their work. Mentioned only by the synoptic writers, these unclean spirits which can possess human beings are expelled by invoking against them the name of God, as in Matt. 7:22. The unclean spirits are not tempters and have no moral direction; their function is simply to cause physical and mental illness by their possession of a person.[11]

The New Testament also speaks of spirits of error which lead the faithful away from the truth.[12] In James 3:15 the believers are warned against a "devilish" wisdom. Rev. 16:14 mentions "demonic spirits" which in the last days will urge kings of the earth to do battle against the divine forces.

Although the New Testament assumes the existence of demons, their occurrence is rarer than in the literature of Judaism.[13] The other important contrast lies in the New Testament's understanding of Satan as the ruler of all demonic forces.

In addition to these specific references to the demonic, the New Testament describes phenomena to which the term *daimonic*, as it is understood in this book, can be applied. These evidences of the daimonic are frequently ambiguous in both origin and effect. They are strong impulses, intuitions, or forces that produce actions which often surprise or bewilder doer and onlooker alike. Sometimes the text attempts an explanation of these evidences of the daimonic; other times no explanation is provided.

One example of this daimonic phenomenon is the celebrated "thorn in the flesh" suffered by Paul the Apostle. Much scholarly speculation has been devoted to the nature of this affliction. Whether Paul was suffering from a physical ailment or from a problem of a different kind, he himself regarded it as a "weakness." The Apostle was ambivalent about the source of his affliction. On the one hand, he understood the "thorn" to be a means for God to help him refrain "from being too elated by the abundance of revelations" (1 Cor. 12:7). Yet, in the same sentence, Paul declared his affliction to be "a messenger of Satan." Although he prayed "three times" for the removal of the thorn, he finally came to terms with it, understanding that the Lord was instructing him through it that divine grace was sufficient for Paul's needs, that God's power "is made perfect in weakness."

The character of Simon Peter reveals evidence of the daimonic at work. In Matt. 16, to Jesus' question to his disciples—"Who do you say that I am?"—Peter answers, "You are the Christ, the Son of the living God." Jesus blesses Peter for this response, declaring that the revelation came not from "flesh and blood," but from "my Father who is in heaven." Immediately afterwards, as Jesus predicts his coming passion, Peter again responds, this time with a rebuke. Jesus turns on Peter with a stinging rebuke of his own: "Get behind me, Satan!" This evidence of the possibility in Peter's daimonic for both good and evil prefigures his denial of Jesus during the trial before the high priest and his later strength of character as recorded in the Acts of the Apostles.

The Gospels point to the presence of the daimonic in Jesus himself. His power over nature revealed itself in the calming of a storm (Mark 6:47 ff.) for the weal of his companions and himself. Yet on another occasion, disappointed that a barren fig tree could not provide food to satisfy his hunger, Jesus cursed it to perpetual barrenness (Mark 11:12–14). The willfulness of Jesus' action is underscored by the Gospel writer, who observes somewhat ruefully that "it was not the season for figs." An attempt later (see Mark 11:20–25) to make a faith lesson out of the incident is a redaction and is not convincing. Jesus' cursing of the fig tree apparently both surprised and confounded his followers.

Mark's Gospel records the curse of the fig tree as an event immediately preceding another evidence of Jesus' daimonic: the casting out of the moneychangers in the temple of Jerusalem. Commentators, in somewhat apologetic terms, have described Jesus' action as "righteous indignation" or "holy anger." That Jesus got angry is made abundantly clear in the Gospel accounts of his denunciations of scribes and Pharisees. The unusual aspect of his anger here is his resorting to violence. Mark places the incident of the moneychangers immediately *before* the cursing of the fig tree, almost as if to excuse Jesus' unjust action against the tree as the aftereffect of his violent actions of the day before in the temple. In Luke, where the fig tree incident is downgraded to a parable (see Luke 13:6–9), the cleansing of the temple is preceded by yet another example of daimonic activity, Jesus' weeping over Jerusalem. The only other time the Gospels mention the tears of Jesus is on the occasion of the death of Lazarus (John 11:35). The bursting forth of emotion, in anger, in tears, in the distress of prayer wrestlings in Gethsemane, in the cry of abandonment from the cross—"My God, my God, why hast thou forsaken me?"—all testify to the presence in Jesus of the phenomenon designated in this study as the daimonic.

The Daimonic in Greek Thought

As we have said, the English word *demon* derives from a Greek word, *daimon*. In Greek thought *daimon* carried an ambiguous meaning. In Homer's *Odyssey*, the characters ascribe numerous mental and physical events to the intervention of nameless daimons or gods. The two terms are used interchangeably. Referring to the *Odyssey*, E. R. Dodds has written:

> Whenever someone has a particularly brilliant or a particularly foolish idea; when he suddenly recognizes another person's identity or sees in a flash the meaning of an omen; when he remembers what he might have forgotten or forgets what he should have remembered, he or someone else will see in it ... a psychic intervention by one of these anonymous supernatural beings.[14]

After the time of Homer, the Greek understanding of daimons gradually underwent change. According to Dodds, daimons began to assume a more persistent, more sinister character. Theognis called hope and fear "dangerous daimons." Sophocles spoke of Eros as a power that "warps to wrong the human mind, for its destruction." Such daimons were thought of as existing outside the person's conscious control; they had a life and energy of their own and could force people into behavior alien to their own wishes.[15] According to another view, a daimon was an endowment at birth which determined one's destiny. If an individual's daimon was of poor quality, no amount of sound judgment could prevent misfortune.

For Socrates, who is often regarded as the supreme rationalist, the daimonic had an important function. It helped persons toward self-realization; it prevented them from a dangerous false optimism in the purely rational. Socrates "took both dreams and oracles very seriously, and . . . habitually heard and obeyed an inner voice which knew more than he did (if we can believe Xenophon, he called it, quite simply, 'the voice of God')."[16]

In his understanding of the daimonic as potentially good, Socrates paved the way for his disciple Plato. For Plato, each person has been endowed with a daimon by God. It serves as the human link with the divine. In Rollo May's words,

> Now we note the *union of good and evil* the Greeks achieved in their concept of the daimon. It is the bridge between the divine and the human, and shares in both. To live in accord with one's daimon (eudaimonism) is difficult but profoundly rewarding. . . . The daimonic destroys purely rationalistic plans and opens the person to creative possibilities he did not know he possessed. It is illustrated by the powerful, snorting horses of Plato's metaphor which require all of a man's strength to control. And though man is never free from this conflict, the struggle gives him a never-failing source of forms and potentialities to awe and to delight him.[17]

CHAPTER II

THE DAIMONIC IN CONTEMPORARY THOUGHT

The Daimonic in Modern Psychology

In his book *Love and Will*, Rollo May offers an introduction to the daimonic as it is treated in contemporary depth psychology. As we have seen, May defines the daimonic as "the urge in every being to affirm itself, assert itself, perpetuate and increase itself."[1] Accordingly, the daimonic can be creative or destructive or both.

On the creative side, the daimonic has much in common with the idea of *genius*. As the Latin rendering of *daimon*, *genius* referred to a deity which guided the destiny of an individual, and later came to mean a particular mental ability. *Genius* also connotes generative power; just so, "the daimonic is the voice of the generative processes within the individual."[2] The daimonic is particularly evident as creativity in the work of poets and artists. In modern fiction, for example, the daimonic has been explored in Herman Hesse's *Steppenwolf*, the novels of Charles Williams, the fantasies of J. R. R. Tolkien and Ursula LeGuin, the stories of Isaac Bashevis Singer and Elie Wiesel, and such novels as *The Magus* by William Fowles and *Sophie's Choice* by William Styron. The poet William Butler Yeats wrote, "And in my heart the daemons and the gods / Wage an eternal battle."[3]

However, the daimonic has a destructive side as well. When it takes over the total self it becomes evil; it becomes possession. It then manifests itself as aggression, hostility, cruelty, "the things about ourselves which horrify us most, and which we repress whenever we can or, more likely, project on others."[4] May sees in Freud's writings a clear perception of the destructive possibilities of the daimonic.

Although Freud seldom referred to the daimonic by name in his works, it is clear that he recognized forces at work in the human psyche that could take over or possess the self. His concept of the libido is of a natural drive that can foil one's most powerful efforts to control it. The various kinds of neuroses and psychoses which Freud courageously explored led him to say of himself, "No one who, like me, conjures up the most evil of those half-tamed demons that inhabit the human breast, and seeks to wrestle with them, can expect to come through the struggle unscathed."[5]

Frued believed that suffering was the destiny of the human race, in consequence of the demands of civilization. Commenting on this rather gloomy Freudian view of human affairs, Douglas N. Morgan finds it at least more realistic than some of the illusory positive-thinking promulgated by the gurus of our time. He agrees with Freud that no " 'art of loving,' no calisthenic healthy-mindedness . . . will ever conceivably bring peace on earth, good will toward men. The reason is blunt and basic: We humans carry within us the seeds of our own destruction, and we nourish them continuously. We must hate as well as love. We will to destroy ourselves and our fellow men, as well as to create and protect them."[6]

Jung and the Shadow

It is in the work of C. G. Jung, however, that the most extensive treatment of the daimonic by a depth psychologist may be found. Departing from Freud, Jung saw in religion not an escape from reality but truths which, if integrated with insights into the human psyche, could lead to wholeness. Jung believed modern culture had produced men and women who were limited by the rational, scientific mode and, as a consequence, cut off from the irrational, uncanny, mysterious aspect of life. It was precisely this part of life, Jung believed, that religion could alone address. After thirty years of dealing with patients, Jung wrote that of those patients over thirty-five, "There has not been one whose problem in the last resort was not that of finding a religious outlook on life. It is safe to say that every one of them fell ill because he had lost what the living religions of every age have given to their followers, and none of them has been healed who did not regain his religious outlook."[7]

Even an elementary understanding of Jung's thought depends upon awareness of a few of his key terms. For Jung the *ego* was the center of consciousness and personal identity; the *self* was a larger entity, that which arouses in persons reverence, fear, and obedience; the *shadow* was the hidden part of the self composed of inferiorities and faults; the *animus* or *anima* was the internal vision of the ideal member of the opposite sex embodying all that is fascinating, disturbing, or endearing about the other sex.[8]

Of particular interest to this study is Jung's understanding of the shadow, because its irrational nature, its hiddenness and darkness, all point to the daimonic. To become conscious of one's shadow, says Jung, "involves recognizing the dark aspects of the personality as present and real." This is no easy task; in fact, it is one from which most people shrink and with good reason, for as people begin to get in touch with the dark, unconscious part of themselves, they discover that this shadow has a "possessive quality."[9] Yet to suppress the shadow is, in the long run, far more dangerous than to acknowledge it and enter into dialogue with it. If the shadow is repressed and isolated from consciousness, it is liable to "burst forth suddenly in a moment of unawareness. The less the shadow is embodied in the individual's conscious life, the blacker and denser it is."[10]

Failure to recognize one's shadow leads a person to project his or her own failings onto others.[11] From this unfortunate circumstance springs the intense hatred of those who are different from oneself. The tension within is turned outward and thereby increases the class, race, and nationalist struggles of the world. For this reason Jung believed an individual fulfilled his or her social responsibility by courageously confronting the shadow within.

> We are convinced that certain people have all the bad qualities we do not know in ourselves or that they practice all those vices which could, of course, never be our own. . . . If you imagine someone who is brave enough to withdraw all these projections, then you get an individual who is conscious of a considerable shadow. Such a man has saddled himself with new problems and conflicts. He has become a serious problem to himself, as he is unable to say that *they* do this or that, *they* are wrong, and *they* must be fought against. . . . Such a man knows that whatever is wrong in the world is in himself, and if he has done something with his own shadow he has done something real for the world. He has succeeded in shouldering at least an infinitesimal part of the gigantic, unsolved social problems of our day.[12]

The shadow, Jung believed, is not to be identified with evil. In fact, it contains qualities which can "vitalize and embellish human existence."[13] Jung taught his patients to personify the shadow in their own lives and enter into dialogue with it in the belief that such conversation would release untapped energy and creativity. To do this, however, Jung taught that the individual must be willing to accept the evil within the self. Acceptance of the self was "the essence of the moral problem."

> That I feed the beggar, that I forgive an insult, that I love my enemy in the name of Christ—all these are undoubtedly great virtues. What I do unto the least of these my brethren, that I do unto Christ. But what if I should discover that the least amongst them all, the poorest of all beggars, the most important of all offenders, yes, the very fiend himself—that these are within me, and that I myself am the enemy who must be loved—what then?[14]

One of Jung's notable contributions, then, was in bringing to light the pervasive dualism of modern culture, a dualism that regards good and evil as irreconcilable opposites, with no relation to each other. For Jung, goodness and evil were inextricably mixed. Evil clings to the purest human motive; human choosing and creating is always clouded by ambiguity.

In *Answer to Job*, an exploration of the problem of evil and God, Jung raised several questions which theologians, as well as all believers, have struggled with. Human understanding, said Jung, sees God's love as limited to giving good gifts to his creatures—"good" as men and women define goodness. But could it be that God has a much broader understanding of good and evil? Could it be that God is working out his divine purposes in ways beyond the common human definitions of goodness? These are questions Jung posed, questions that have both psychological and theological implications. Jung compared his theological view of God with that of an early church father, Clement of Rome, who taught "that God rules the world with a right and a left hand, the right being Christ, the left Satan. Clement's view is clearly *monotheistic*, as it unites the opposites in one God."[15]

Jung saw irrationality in God, just as he saw it in humanity. Failure to recognize this dimension in both, he believed, was tragic.

Transforming the Daimonic

In her essay, "The Psychological Reality of the Demonic," Ann Ulanov describes the demonic as an "adversary," but an adversary that can be transformed either into one's "advocate" or into "an antagonist unalterably opposed to human concerns." In the first instance, the demonic as advocate comes as something other than oneself pleading for a wider perspective than an ego-centered point of view. It is a "vital force" whose aim is not to disrupt or destroy but to offer "a deeper perception, a more passionate relationship to something beyond the ego."[16] Ulanov compares the demon as advocate with Jung's description of the "right conscience": "an autonomous dynamism, fittingly called man's daemon, genius, guardian angel, better self, heart, inner voice."[17] The second kind of adversary, the demonic as antagonist, is characterized by darkness, density, and even malevolence. Here Jung's description of the shadow is appropriate.

Whether the demonic appears as advocate or antagonist, the individual must try to see it and come to terms with it. Refusal to do so results in either possession by the demonic or repression of it. Both have serious negative consequences.

Possession by the demonic, as Ulanov defines it, means that the conscious personality is invaded and captured by the demonic element. Any natural part of the psyche can assume demonic form. The ego, instead of asserting one's own thoughts, plans, and possibilities, is taken over by the unconscious. There is no personal standpoint to withstand the invasion of unconscious elements. Invaded by the demonic, one is compelled to act out its wishes, in spite of formerly held values. One is driven to extremes of lust, hatred, and violence.[18]

In repression of the demonic, on the other hand, the individual pushes it down into the unconscious, where it is "free to roam wherever it pleases, free to mix with anything else that dwells in the unconscious, becoming more and more undifferentiated." When the repressed demonic is released, it most often takes the form of projection.[19]

Ulanov stresses the importance of bringing the demonic into consciousness. The shadow elements of the personality are not necessarily destructive. They may turn out to be "advocates of the wider, deeper self, but initially they are always ambivalent." If one turns away from the demonic, there is no channel available for its positive transformation or integration into consciousness. For Ulanov, the important word in relation to the demonic is *respect*. She warns that frivolous curiosity or naive optimism regarding the demonic is a dangerous error. However, Ulanov, though she writes of the possibility of transforming the demonic, touches only briefly on the subject in her essay. She describes the dreams of some of her clients and seems to suggest that understanding one's dreams can be of help. She states that "consciousness is an indispensable ingredient in the transformation process of the demonic," but that consciousness itself is not enough.[20]

Rollo May offers some possibilities for transforming the demonic, though May himself prefers the word *daimonic*. He posits three stages of the daimonic. First is the *impersonal* stage, in which "we ... experience the daimonic as a blind push, driving us toward the assertion of ourselves," as in rage or sex.[21] In Freudian vocabulary, the daimonic experienced at this level is the *id*. It is impersonal in the sense that it places no value on particular persons or ideas. At this stage the destructive possibilities of the daimonic are greatest.

The next stage is that of the *personal*. By deepening and widening consciousness, one channels the daimonic so it becomes individualized and personalized. Here human choice enters the picture. Sexual appetite, for instance, is channeled into a desire to make love to, and be loved by, the person one chooses. As one becomes conscious of the daimonic in the self, one can exert some control over it. "Thus, the daimonic becomes the personal daimon, the particular pattern of being which constitutes my own center."[22] One important means of making the daimonic personal lies in naming it. May finds it significant that the Bible ascribes importance to the naming function, as in Adam's naming of the animals in Genesis and Jesus' naming the demons in order to cast them out. Naming allows one to enter into personal dialogue with the daimonic.

In such a dialogue, one is pushed toward the *logos*, which May defines as "the meaningful structure of reality."[23] One thus approaches the third and highest stage of the daimonic, the *transpersonal*. In this stage the daimonic aids one in expanding the interpersonal meaning of one's life. Ethically, it is to appeal to the principle of universality: would this way of acting, if adopted by other people, lead to the greater benefit of all?

The Daimonic in the Theology of Paul Tillich

More than any other theologian of the present century, it was Paul Tillich who took into account the role of the daimonic. In an essay published in 1925, Tillich saw a polarity in the Holy consisting of the "divine" and the "demonic." "The demonic is the Holy (or the sacred) with a minus sign before it, the sacred antidivine."[24] But Tillich found dualism in religion to be untenable; a religious dualism which concentrated divine holiness in one realm and demonic holiness in another realm results, in Tillich's view, in a false picture of reality.

Another essay by Tillich, "The Demonic," was published a year later in 1926 as part of his larger work, *The Interpretation of History*. Here Tillich spoke of the dialectical quality of the demonic. Just as earlier Tillich saw a polarity in the Holy, in this essay he described a polarity within the demonic; it contains both "form-creating and form-destroying strength."[25] Affirmation of the existence of the demonic has nothing to do with a mythological or metaphysical affirmation of the world of spirits. To thus objectify the demonic would strip it of its dialectical nature.

In a discussion of the effect of the demonic on personality, Tillich used the term "possession" to describe the demonic's

successful attack on the freedom and unity of human consciousness. One's ego is taken over by that which is outside it,
the demonic. Tillich did not identify the demonic with the
unconscious, however. "Psychologically, the demonic belongs
just as much to the subconscious, from which it originates, as
to the conscious, into which it pours."[26] The demonic has an
ecstatic, overpowering, original quality, although in the end it
can destroy the ego which it has possessed.

Tillich contrasted the state of demonic possession to the state
of grace. In both cases, powerful, original forces break into
consciousness. Ultimately, however, grace ("divine ecstasy")
brings about an elevation of being, "of creative and formative
power; the demonic ecstasy brings about weakening of being,
disintegration and decay." Demonic inspiration does indeed
reveal the divine, but as "a reality which it fears, which it
cannot love, with which it cannot unite."[27]

In this same seminal essay, Tillich wrote of the relationship
of the demonic to sin. He said that stripping the concept of sin
of its demonic property results in the inadequate, moralistic
view of Enlightenment thinkers.

> The demonic is the perversion of the creative, and as such
> belongs to the phenomena that are contrary to essential
> nature, or sin. In the creative in itself the demonic is bot-
> tom and depth, but it does not break out as demonic.[28]

Tillich illustrated how the demonic perverts the creative in
a discussion of the human view of God. Traditionally, distrust
of God is regarded as the root of sin. Where does this distrust
come from? From "the demonization of God in human consciousness." One dare not surrender to God because one sees
only God's "absolute claim and rejecting wrath." The divine
thus wears a purely demonic aspect. In experiencing this terrible view of God as a demon, one cannot be in relationship with
God.

Outside of grace, God is a law, a judgment which drives one to despair. He becomes God—in contrast to the demon—through grace. That is the deepest relation of sin and demonry.[29]

If one considers the historical situation in which Tillich was living when he wrote his essay on the demonic, one can understand the depth of his concern. In a later essay, "On the Boundary," published in 1936, Tillich described the demonic as "something finite, something limited, which puts on infinite, unlimited dignity."[30] In that sentence, as in his earlier essay, one can discern the spectre of Tillich's homeland in which the demonic had erupted with devastating effect.

In his later writings, Tillich spoke of "the courage to take the anxiety of the demonic upon oneself," "to affirm one's own demonic depth," and of the discovery of "the demonic as the ambiguous ground of the creative."[31] And in the third volume of his *Systematic Theology*, Tillich described "an element of chaos" which seems to echo his earlier understanding of the demonic. Chaos, said Tillich, cannot be understood apart from creation, to which it belongs. In the life of the creature, as opposed to the divine life, "chaos leads to the ambiguity of self-creativity and destructiveness. . . . In every process of life structures of creation are mixed with powers of destruction in such a way that they cannot be unambiguously separated."[32]

Later in the same volume, in his discussion of the ambiguities of religion, Tillich lamented the fact that discussion of the demonic in theological circles so frequently designates only the "antidivine forces in individual and social life." Thus the ambiguous character of the demonic is brushed aside. Just as in mythological thought demons are not simply negations of the divine but participants in the power and holiness of the divine, so the demonic in every age participates in the divine by identifying a particular bearer of the Holy with the Holy itself. The characteristic of the demonic is "the claim of something finite to infinity or divine greatness."[33]

Within the individual personality, the demonic manifests itself as internal conflicts that have integrating as well as disintegrating, creative as well as destructive consequences.[34] Unambiguous life is forever sought but can never be realized. And this means that in existence, the demonic cannot finally be avoided or eliminated.

> It is an age-old experience of all religions that the quest for something transcending them is answered in the shaking and transforming experiences of revelation and salvation; but that under the conditions of existence even the absolutely great—the divine self-manifestation—becomes not only great but also small, not only divine but also demonic.[35]

The Daimonic in the Fantasy Fiction of Ursula K. LeGuin

In 1972 *A Wizard of Earthsea* by Ursula K. LeGuin was awarded the National Book Award for Children's Literature. The first volume of what came to be named *The Earthsea Trilogy*, is an example of what has been called by one critic "ethical fantasy." By this is meant stories for children that intend to teach as well as to please, but that do so in nondidactic fashion. Ethical fantasy presupposes a world enmeshed in "a vast struggle between Right and Wrong, Good and Evil, or grievously periled by an unexpected shift in equilibrium between Light and Dark, Balance and Imbalance."[36] Authors who have gained prominence for this kind of writing are George MacDonald, C. S. Lewis, and Madeleine L'Engle, to name a few.

Ursula LeGuin is best known for her adult science fiction. In recent years, however, she has moved out of that genre into the wider field of fantasy. In an interview she once said: "When in difficulties [in writing] I fall back into my native tongue, which is that of non-intellectualized fantasy, daydreams, symbol, myth."[37] Her use of this "native tongue" is revealed most clearly in *The Earthsea Trilogy*. Although LeGuin acknowledges that the trilogy was indeed written for children, she expresses frustration that many adults therefore write it off as insignificant. She characterizes such patronizing attitudes as "adult chauvinist piggery."[38] Of the first volume of the trilogy she writes: "The most childish thing about *A Wizard of Earth Sea*, I expect, is its subject: coming of age."[39] "Coming of age" may indeed be the "subject" of this novel, but its characters and story are more reminiscent of ancient myth than of typical adolescent fiction.

The main character first appears as seven year old Duny, "a tall, quick boy, loud and proud and full of temper."[40] He learns that he has special powers in casting spells, powers that bring him to the attention of the mage or wizard named Ogion the Silent. Under his apprenticeship, Duny begins his study of wizardry and receives his true name, Ged. This name stands in contrast to the popular name of Sparrowhawk accorded him by the villagers.

Soon there appears in Ged a conflict between the love of learning and a desire for power. In a forbidden book of lore, he comes across a spell for summoning spirits from the dead. As he reads, an ominous darkness enters the room and seems to solidify. Ogion disperses the form and warns Ged that wizardry has ethical dimensions. "Think of this: that every word, every act of our Art is said and is done either for good, or for evil. Before you speak or do you must know the price that is to pay!"[41]

As he continues his study in the years that follow, Ged is lured by the prospect of unlimited power. He dreams of controlling the balance between light and darkness. Responding to the taunts of a rival, he boasts that "by my name" he will summon a spirit from the dead. In the act of summoning, he falls forward on the earth. Then a breach in "the fabric of the world" opens and a terrible brightness appears; out of it springs a "clot of black shadow." It leaps upon Ged and nearly kills the young wizard.

Surviving the attack, Ged determines to undo the evil he has perpetrated. He continues his studies and then begins work as a mage. The shadow he has unleashed, however, haunts all his activity. It pursues him through various deeds of prowess and kindness that reveal a growing strength of character. Finally he realizes that he cannot run from the shadow any longer. Although he fears the confrontation, he sets out to track down his nemesis. His quest takes him beyond the last island in the East Reach where land and sea are replaced by earthsea.

At last the two come to their final encounter. The shadow approaches, first shapeless; then it changes into the shapes of all those people in Ged's life on whom he had projected his hates and fears. Finally it appears as it did at first, "crawling on four taloned legs upon the sand." Then it heaves itself upright, and in silence, man and shadow meet face to face.

> Aloud and clearly, breaking that old silence, Ged spoke the shadow's name and in the same moment the shadow spoke without lips or tongue, saying the same word: "Ged." And the two voices were one voice.
>
> Ged reached out his hands, dropping his staff, and took hold of the shadow, of the black self that reached out to him. Light and darkness met, and joined, and were one.[42]

In a perceptive commentary on this novel, Rollin A. Lasseter notes the importance of Ged's names and the naming of the shadow. Only by finding, holding, naming the unnamed and unloved in us can we redeem it. We must know "what thing from unlife" the shadow corresponds to and belongs to. All things have a name, as Ged discovered. Like him, we must name our own shadow, says Lasseter.[43]

The shadow in *A Wizard of Earthsea* sounds very much like Jung's; indeed, in an essay entitled "The Child and the Shadow,"

LeGuin defends fantasy written for children by appealing to Jung's use of the shadow. After summarizing some of Jung's basic ideas, she offers her own understanding of the shadow. It "is not simply evil." It is "inferior, primitive, awkward, animallike, childlike; powerful, vital, spontaneous." Without it, LeGuin says, "the person is nothing."[44]

LeGuin perceives adolescence to be a time of internal conflict. Normal adolescents shoulder a heavy load of guilt as they begin to take responsibility for their own actions. They see their shadow as darker than it really is. The only way for a youngster to get past the immobilizing self-blame of this stage "is really to look at that shadow, to face it, warts and fangs and pimples and claws and all—to accept it as himself—as *part* of himself."[45]

That, of course, is exactly what the adolescent Ged accomplishes in *A Wizard of Earthsea*. LeGuin argues that fantasy is best suited to describe the inward journey, the "voyage into the unconscious," that the adolescent needs to make. By facing his own shadow, he can grow up to adulthood less inclined "either to give up in despair or to deny what he sees," when he must face the evil that undeniably exists in the world "and the injustices and grief and suffering that we all must bear, and the final shadow at the end of all."[46]

Fantasy, LeGuin admits, plays loose with the facts, but it is *true*. Children know it and love it. Adults know it and fear it. They know that the truth of fantasy "challenges, even threatens, all that is false, all that is phony, unnecessary, and trivial" in the life they have allowed themselves to be boxed into. They are "afraid of dragons, because they are afraid of freedom."[47]

LeGuin recognizes the limitations of fantasy. She identifies its primary danger as that of extreme introversion. Left to itself, fantasy may remain entirely private to the fantastist's consciousness, or even remain unconscious, like a dream. The danger is real, as Ged himself recognized. Counseled by Ogion, his wizard mentor, that he should "seek what seeks you . . . hunt the hunger," Ged replies, "if it defeats me wholly . . . it will take my knowledge and my power, and use them."[48] The danger is not only to the self. "It threatens only me, now. But if it enters into me and possesses me, it will work great evil through me."[49]

For all its danger, entry into the world of the imagination, which is the unconscious, with its dragons and shadows and monsters, is greatly to be preferred to rejection of it. LeGuin says that people who are threatened by it usually dismiss it as childish. The dismissal is to be much regretted, says LeGuin, but the description is on the mark.

> In the creation and preservation of fantasy worlds, the role of the child seems central.
>   The politician, the profiteer, and the sensualist have no patience with the other-worldly. The other world . . . Jesus referred to it in its religious aspect when he remarked that access to it was limited to those willing to become little children. The kingdom of God is within you; the burning-ground where the goddess dances is the heart.[50]

A Summation

There are several common threads running through the writings in psychology, theology, and fiction examined in this chapter. One theme is the *ambiguity* that characterizes the daimonic. It is a mistake to identify the daimonic as purely evil. To do so would lead one to try to deny or annihilate it, and such efforts result eventually in the violent, destructive eruption of the daimonic.

If the daimonic is not wholly evil, then what *possibilities for good* does it offer? For Jung, such possibilities inhere in the acceptance of the self and the end that brings to the evils of projection. Tillich saw in the daimonic the necessary ingredient for creativity. LeGuin speaks in terms of maturation, coming of age.

But the daimonic is not to be taken lightly, nor approached in a prideful spirit. Jung and May, Tillich and LeGuin all acknowledge the terrifying *possibility of possession* by the daimonic. When a person or a group is taken over by the daimonic, the possible destruction is great indeed. Terrors are set loose which will expend themselves in devastation of the human mind and body, of the human community, of the natural world.

Another common theme is that of the *mythical language* employed in the discussion of the daimonic. Psychologist, theologian, and artist naturally resort to their distinctive vocabularies in an attempt to define the indefinable. It is hardly surprising to discover that they frequently resort to symbols as well. They speak of light and darkness, of shadows, of monsters and demons, of bottom and depth. None of their descriptions is exact. They cannot be, given the irrational nature of the daimonic.

It is interesting to note, also, that Jung, Tillich, and LeGuin are all regarded with some suspicion in their respective fields. None of them quite fits into the mainstream. Jung is suspect because he ventured into areas rather far afield from the usual concerns of psychology. Tillich, while acknowledged as a brilliant intellectual, comes too close to atheism for the orthodox. LeGuin, until very recently, was given little critical attention because her writing has been categorized as science fiction or children's literature, neither of which has been regarded by the critics as "serious literature."

Finally, what all three have in common is the conviction that *confronting the daimonic is imperative*. Wholeness, health, salvation, maturity can not be achieved without it. The dangers in facing the daimonic are great, but failure to do so is even more dangerous. In a century in which the rational side of humanity has been given almost exclusive veneration, the outbreaks of the irrational in wars, genocide, and despoliation of the earth have been unparalleled in human history. The voices of those who courageously call their fellows to confront the daimonic, and there have been all too few, are thus of no little significance. Failure to heed them may yet lead to cataclysm.

THE PREACHING TASK

Critiques of Preaching

Much has been written on the subject of preaching. In the past, books about preaching dealt primarily with the hermeneutical function or the homiletical form. Advice was given to aspiring preachers on how to study the biblical text and then how to apply it to the practical experience of the listeners in sermon form. As Richard A. Jensen has noted, this division between hermeneutics and homiletics lays a tremendous burden on the preacher. Drawing on the theological thought of Gustaf Wingren, Jensen writes that

> we have not understood the indispensable connection between God's word and human life. We have tended to see these realities as having an *independent* existence. . . . The task facing the preacher has traditionally been thought of as bringing these two independently existing realities into relationship with each other in the sermon.[1]

The preacher was aided in the homiletical part of his or her task, however, by books which gave instruction on how to build a sermon. The verb *build* is chosen expressly because the creating of sermons was frequently envisioned as a construction process. One started with the blueprint or outline, which was supposed to contain an introduction, three major headings, and a conclusion. The next step was to fill out this framework with such furnishings as commentary on the text, illustrations, and transitional statements. Finally, one was to give close attention to the choice of appropriate words and phrases.

In the past several years, a number of books have appeared which call into question this classic approach to preaching. Indebted to the insights of Marshall McLuhan, one critic of contemporary preaching, Clyde Fant, has decried the long lasting influence of nineteenth century preachers who were literary craftsmen. As a result, he says, preachers were taught to write sermons in a style more suited for reading than for hearing. "Like a satellite trapped within the gravitational pull of a planet, preaching has been locked into the Gutenberg galaxy. The sermon must break out of this orbit if it is to be able to communicate within its own medium."[2]

Others have taken up this theme and hopefully predict that preaching will soon be freed from the straitjacket of the three points and a conclusion format.[3] Fred B. Craddock has gained deserved prominence for his advocacy of the inductive method of preaching. In his analysis of contemporary preaching, Craddock notes the continuing popularity of the traditional deductive method. This method consists of stating the thesis, dividing into points or sub-theses, explaining and illustrating these points, and finally drawing out of them practical applications for the listeners. In this arrangement, the conclusion (thesis) precedes the development.

As Craddock points out, the deductive method of preaching presupposes a situation in which the speaker is the acknowledged authority with the right, even duty, to impart truth to the listeners. Such a presupposition doubtless was relevant for as long as the Western world, at least, was synonymous with Christendom. That day, needless to say, has long since passed. Today dialogue, not monologue, is needed in preaching. The congregation will no longer be content to exist merely as the receiver of truth.

A second objection Craddock has to the deductive method lies in its essentially static nature. The lack of movement is evident as the preacher attempts to proceed through the sermon according to the proposed outline. "How does one get from 2b to main point II?" asks Craddock. "The limp phrase, 'Now in the second place,' hardly has the leverage. He who has had the nerve to cast a critical eye on his old sermons has probably discovered that some sermons were three sermonettes barely glued together."[4]

As an alternative to the deductive method of preaching, Craddock commends induction. The movement in an inductive sermon is from the particulars of experience to or at least towards a general truth or conclusion. The method of induction in preaching is more descriptive than prescriptive. It allows the listeners to make applications of the sermon for themselves. By using the inductive method, preachers will realize that they are speaking not only *to* the listeners but *for* them. Preaching is not seen as bringing the truth of God to ignorant souls, but rather as an entry into conversation with people who have already been asking questions about ultimate reality and have begun to find some answers. By acknowledging their shared humanity with the listeners, preachers will be less likely to "talk down" to them. Particular life experiences are thus a primary ingredient of the inductive sermon. On the basis of such experiences, along with the listeners' identification with what they hear, "conclusions are reached, new perspectives gained, decisions made."[5]

The inductive method has the advantage of natural movement; it proceeds from the known to the unknown. Craddock compares the movement of an inductive sermon to that of a story. Such movement creates and sustains interest by rousing in the listeners a sense of anticipation. The Bible reveals a continuous tension between the "already" and the "not yet," and an inductive sermon helps the listeners be in touch with this reality in their own lives. An inductive sermon can thus be characterized as "moving, open and expectant."[6]

Eugene Lowry has also objected to sermons as pieces of deductive logic. He recalls what most high school and college students can recall: the principles of outlining which stressed how various sub-points needed to be parallel to each other and equally subservient to the larger point. A completed outline, if constructed "correctly," gave the appearance of a blueprint of organized ideas, all fitted together with a logic that concentrated on the relationship of parts to the whole. As Lowry notes, sermons which come into being by the outline approach will inevitably feature substance over movement.

> This viewpoint will impel us toward organizing sermons on the basis of the logic of their ideational ingredients. But a sermon is not a logical assemblage; a sermon is an event-in-time which follows the logic born of the communication interaction between preacher and congregation. To organize on the basis of the logic of ideational ingredients is to miss altogether the dynamics of that communicational reality.[7]

What is the alternative? Lowry proposes that preachers stop thinking in terms of "constructing" a sermon, stop perceiving themselves as engineers or architects in need of blueprints (outlines), and begin instead to view preaching as an art form and themselves as artists. Preaching, according to Lowry, is essentially *storytelling*, and a sermon is a narrative art form.[8]

Another articulate spokesman for this view of the story as paradigm for preaching has been Charles L. Rice. In his book *Interpretation and Imagination*, Rice raised the question of what homiletical form was appropriate to telling the good news of the word of God. His answer was that it is much easier to say what that form is *not*: "didactic, propositional, stereotyped, woodenly textual, moralistically categorical." Trying to articulate what the form should be, however, proved more difficult. "A positive reconstruction will necessarily remain unconstructed, relying upon impressions of a given situation, inventiveness, spontaneous innovation."[9]

Ten years later, Rice could be more definite about the form preaching should take. "At the most profound level of symbolization — where experience becomes meaningful — we relate our stories to *the Story*. If we were pressed to say what Christian faith and life are, we could hardly do better than *hearing, telling and living a story*. And if asked for a short definition of preaching could we do better than *shared story?*"[10] In the volume from which this quotation is taken, several homilists offer their commentaries on this view of preaching as shared story, story being considered from the standpoint of the preacher, the listener, and the message.

Eugene Lowry offers a particularly helpful analysis of the sermon as story or, in his own words, as "a narrative art form." An important element in any story is plot. The plot of a sermon will have as its key ingredient "a sensed discrepancy, a homiletical bind. Something is 'up in the air' — an issue not resolved."[11] Because Lowry sees the sermon as an event existing in time rather than a thing existing in space, as process rather than as collection of parts, he encourages the preacher to begin creating the sermon by thinking in terms of sequence rather than structure. The stages in this sequence make up what Lowry calls "the homiletical plot."

Lowry identifies five stages in the homiletical plot. The first stage is "upsetting the equilibrium." By this is meant drawing the listeners into the ambiguity, the anxiety of human experience. People in the congregation will often need help in preparing themselves to hear the gospel. The creation of disequilibrium is necessary for the process to begin. The second stage, "analyzing the discrepancy," is often the most lengthy in terms of the time it occupies in the sermon itself. Here the question *why?* is central. An analysis of the ambiguity of the human condition follows, one that is sufficiently thorough to avoid both simplistic diagnosis and simplistic remedies. "Disclosing the clue to the resolution" is the third stage in Lowry's homiletical plot. Here the principle of "reversal" comes into play, a reversal found in the radical discontinuity between worldly wisdom and the gospel. The fourth stage, "experiencing the gospel," announces the good news of God's salvation. Lowry notes that most preachers are in a great hurry to get to this stage without having given serious enough attention to the previous stages. The fifth stage is named "anticipating the consequences." It includes the invitation to receive the grace of God and to move forward into newness of life.

What the view of sermon as story and, in particular, Lowry's description of the homiletical plot make possible is an understanding of preaching as a dynamic process. Such an understanding allows the preacher to see sermon preparation more as an opportunity for exploration and discovery (often *surprising* discovery) and less a task of researching, organizing, and presenting. The homiletical plot, as Lowry describes it, is also what happens to the preacher prior to or along with the creation of the sermon. In a sense, what preachers do in creating a sermon is to recapture the stages of struggle and discovery that they have already undergone. Preaching, therefore, will reveal movement and "plot" and a dynamic quality only to the extent that these elements are at work within the person of the preacher.

There is, of course, a real danger in focusing too much attention on the preacher. All the risks of egotism, pride, and self-righteousness loom immediately. The preacher as person must never be thought of as the starting point. The scripture text, the tradition, the living word of God — these are the starting points. Yet the contemporary meaning of the tradition cannot be imparted in worship without the preacher. The preacher is the point where ancient text and modern congregation come together. In an incarnational religion such as Christianity, the risks must therefore always be recognized, but must also always be taken!

Addressing this issue, Hans van der Geest, in a book with the provocative subtitle, *The Impact of Personality in Preaching*, argues that one is able to preach "personally," to awaken deep experiences in others, only if one is able to reach oneself and accept oneself. He counsels preachers to seek access to their own interiors, interiors which at first glance appear comical, childish, not really ready to be shown in public. But this contact with the self is of "decisive importance" in preparing a sermon. The idea for the sermon emerges only in "a creative restlessness," when the preacher dares to ignore the constricting patterns of thought acquired early in life. Van der Geest says of preachers:

> Precisely the thing they are suppressing inside ends up having an effect on the listeners, and this is what is tragic about suppression. It has an effect on others without our wanting it to, and does so much more strongly than we think is possible. That suppressed element becomes autonomous, slips from our control and takes on a demonic power.[12]

Among contemporary preachers, few have argued as persuasively for preachers to speak out of the depth of their own life experiences as has Frederick Buechner. He faults much preaching today as being shallow, filled with "interesting little things" that preachers have stumbled across in their reading. He finds many preachers saying things that do not "speak out of anything really important to them or to anything really important to them."[13] Buechner's special gift, whether in his novels, autobiography, lectures on preaching, or his sermons, is his ability to make connections between the biblical word and the depths of his own life story. Few preachers have the poetic gifts he does, but that is not the point. Every preacher can benefit by heeding the counsel Buechner gives: "Listen to your life." Preachers whose sermons are often lifeless, sterile, harmless homilies can find renewal for themselves and their congregations by allowing the biblical story to be in dialogue with their own stories. As Buechner puts it: "Drawing on nothing fancier than the poetry of his own life, let [the preacher] use words and images that help make the surface of our lives transparent to the truth that lies deep within them, which is the wordless truth of who we are and who God is and the Gospel of our meeting."[14]

A Personal Critique

At this point we have come to a watershed. Thus far, the exploration has been cast in the form of objective inquiry. However, because of my own personal involvement in preaching and the necessity of drawing upon that involvement for what follows, I shall, for much of the remainder of this book, resort to speaking in the first person. I do so at this precise point because I have found the understanding of preaching as story shared through the person of the preacher to be extremely valuable in my own vocation.

Looking back on my sermons after graduation from seminary, I discover that for the first three months in the pulpit, I used as texts the narratives in Genesis. Those sermons told the stories of Adam and Eve, Cain and Abel, Noah, Abraham, Isaac, and the rest. All this predated the theologies of story which have become so fashionable in the past decade. Perhaps it was intuition that guided me in those early years of preaching; more likely it was my own love of stories since childhood.[15] Whatever the reason, I ignored, not without some feelings of guilt, the urging of the homiletical textbooks to be faithful to the standard three-point sermon model. Only rarely, in fact, have I consciously attempted to follow that prescribed pattern.

It was therefore, more than a little gratifying when theologians, biblical scholars, and professors of homiletics began writing books on the necessity for preaching to be shaped by the paradigm of story. It was good to have been right all along, even if I was not aware of it! I must hasten to add, however, that my preaching is markedly different today from fourteen years ago, even though telling the story of God's redeeming love continues to be my own understanding of the preaching task. My preaching has been greatly strengthened by acquaintance with many of the excellent works published on the role of story in both faith and proclamation.[16] Of equal importance has been my ongoing dialogue with films, drama, and fiction, both historical and contemporary. These varied resources have helped me become more aware of the human condition in myself and in others and to learn some of the skills of the storyteller. As a representative example of such resources, I cite the following, written by two parish pastors.

> When my hearers sense that a part of the biblical story has indeed become *my* story, they are invited to make connections with their own stories. They are not compelled to enter into what is happening for me, and there can be no guarantee that they will. But seeing and hearing, in their preacher, a living person who is in touch with real feelings and who is actually experiencing connections between God's ongoing Story and his own gives them example and encouragement and hope.[17]

I find such words to be both instructive and encouraging, just as I do much of what is being written about preaching these days. And yet. . .

There is a dimension to preaching, even when it is conceived of primarily as telling the story, that I find conspicuously absent; namely, what happens to the preacher in the process? It is encouraging to be told, "Simply tell the story. Tell the story simply."[18] It is inspiring to be admonished:

> Let the preacher tell the truth. . . . Let him preach this overwhelming of tragedy by comedy, of darkness by light, of the ordinary by the extraordinary, as the tale that is too good not to be true because to dismiss it as untrue is to

dismiss along with it that catch of the breath, that beat and lifting of the heart near to or even accompanied by tears, which I believe is the deepest intuition of truth we have.[19]

But can the preacher be blamed if he or she asks: how am I to go about telling the story, telling the truth? How do the raw materials of biblical exegesis, thinking, praying, writing, and oral delivery get translated into a telling of the story that has the power to transform lives? The answer, of course, is wrapped in mystery, the mystery of transcendence. The orthodox will speak of the Holy Spirit. And that may be as close to an accurate description as one can get.

Yet it is my contention that inquiry into the process of *creating* yields some important insights for those of us who are faced with the critical task of telling the story. Many recent in-depth studies of human creativity avoid religious language. Writers on the subject prefer to use the vocabulary of aesthetics, phenomenology, or psychology.[20] There is a dearth of material on the relationship of creativity and Christian faith.

A well-known exception has been Dorothy Sayers' *The Mind of the Maker*. In that book, Sayers applied the Christian doctrine of the trinity to the process involved in the creation of a literary work. Her aim was to demonstrate that statements in Christian creeds about the "Mind of the Divine Maker" represent true statements about the mind of the human maker— the artist.[21] She asserted that the three persons of the trinity coincide with the three ingredients in the creative process. The Idea, which corresponds to the first person, precedes the mental or physical work of the artist and gives order to the activity of creation. Energy, the second person in Sayers' trinitarian structure, is the sum and process of all the activity which bring a work into temporal and spatial existence. The third person is Power—that which flows back to the writer from his or her own activity and likewise is the means whereby the Energy and Idea are communicated to the reader.[22]

The Mind of the Maker offers a helpful way of understanding the creative experience. Like the artist, the preacher can appreciate the crucial relationship between the first and second persons in Sayers' trinity: the movement from Idea to Energy, giving form to the idea. The preacher can sympathize with the dilemma of the poet Stephen Spender, who writes of why it is so much easier for him to explain what he wants to write rather than actually to write it:

> How difficult it would be to write it. For writing it would imply living my way through the imaged experience of all these ideas, which are here mere abstractions, and such an effort of imaginative experience requires a lifetime of patience and watching.[23]

Of the preacher too is required a "lifetime of patience and watching." But the preacher does not have the luxury of not producing. Sunday follows Sunday and the congregation waits for the Word to be enfleshed, the story to be told.

Nevertheless, there is a kinship between the artist and the preacher. The creative process is common to both. In her book, *Creative Preaching: Finding the Words*, Elizabeth Achtemeier devotes a chapter to the nature and development of creativity. In it she focuses attention on the importance of language and does so by frequent reference to the work of literary artists. Both preacher and artist use the same tools: words. Preachers will benefit, therefore, by reading and studying the great writers. The study of language is "an inexpendable pursuit." Preachers will learn to write well by reading well, to speak well by listening to great language from novelists, dramatists, poets, historians, essayists, biographers, and artistic preachers. Preachers should read in order to absorb the rhythms and nuances of language; but Achtemeier urges preachers to read also to "know the world," to "grow as human beings," to learn the "fine art of communication." Preaching is "artistry—the practice of fine art." Yet it is never art for art's sake; the goal is always the communication of the gospel. Therefore the preacher must draw on the creative resources of discipline and devotion.[24]

In the end, Achtemeier despairs of the task of saying what it means to preach creatively. On the last page of her book, she falls back on religious language to make up for the deficiency of her study. Study disciplines, homiletical principles, methods of exegesis and style are "not sufficient."

> Creative preaching finally happens only when God in Christ lays hold of our lives and works his transforming new creation in heart and mind and action. Then words catch fire, and love is born, and the Christian community becomes reality....[25]

While one can acknowledge and even affirm the sincere piety of these words, they also point to the inadequacy of Achtemeier's study. If, finally, we can offer no more on the subject of creative preaching than faith confession, we have followed a circular path.

A study which probes more deeply into the creative process as it relates to preaching is a book by Robert D. Young. Drawing on his own experience as a parish preacher, Young writes of the place of the "religious imagination" in the preacher's work. He uses as his model the Old Testament seers.

> In early days, these seers looked at prosaic two-plus-two's, and saw enormous amounts.... They found hidden connections between the tradition and their times, and the lines went back to God, and forward into some kingdom to come. They were seers who used those frail things called words, whereby they transported ideas, and conveyed directions. That is the tradition in which I stand.[26]

Young goes on to explore the biblical and theological dimensions of creativity and then to apply his findings to the weekly task of preaching. His study has the merit of being grounded in the reality of pastoral experience. It is particularly helpful when it compares the creative process as experienced by artists, poets, and novelists with what can happen in the creative work in which a preacher engages. From my own perspective, Young's critical shortcoming is his tendency to romanticize the creative experience. He acknowledges that creativity calls for hard work, and he spends his final chapter giving a kind of pep talk to preachers who hesitate to give rein to their creative impulses. He discusses five rewards for the seer: a new sense of creation, a new sense of freedom, a new sense of self-worth and identity, a new sense of the Holy Spirit's work, and a new power to motivate. His comments are encouraging. But it all sounds too good to be true. We discovered in Chapter II that the creative impulse is the other side of the destructive impulse. Young fails to see that relationship. As helpful as his book is, it does not cut deeply enough because it does not acknowledge the daimonic.

Nor, it must be said, do other studies, even thorough ones, on the subject of preaching. Not only is the daimonic never mentioned by name, there is likewise a nearly universal absence of the *idea* of the daimonic in such studies. Why? Present-day Christian theology has little time for themes related to either the daimonic or the demonic. Even Paul Tillich, whose writings on the subject were summarized above, seems, in his later years, to have assigned to the demonic a minor role in his thought.

Paradoxically, studies on the origin and nature of evil continue to pour forth. They range from the popularized approach of the best seller *When Bad Things Happen to Good People* by Rabbi Harold Kushner, to complex philosophical and theological treatises. Those whose scholarly task it is to provide a Christian apologetic for preaching, however, are not likely to turn for source material to books on the subject of evil. Instead, they concentrate on hermeneutics or on preaching methodology. Necessary as both these disciplines are, they fail to account for the dialectical nature of the creative process in preaching, or for the daimonic factor in that process.

For example, two influential books on preaching by Fred B. Craddock—*As One Without Authority* and *Overhearing the Gospel*—are devoted to the subject of preaching methods. Both offer creative ideas, both build on solid theological foundations. And, in the latter, the dialectical thought of Soren Kierkegaard is cited as authoritative. Reading these two books, any alert preacher will be helped in the direction of creativity *in terms of preaching method*. But what happens inside the preacher to help or hinder creativity? The issue is not addressed adequately.

The same can be said of a book like Eugene Lowry's *The Homiletical Plot: The Sermon as Narrative Art Form*. Lowry's thesis is provocative and of potentially great benefit to the preacher. But again, little is said about the creative process taking place within the person of the preacher. The noting of this omission is not intended as an indictment of the author. I mention it simply to call attention to the absence of discussion about a subject that I believe to be of heretofore unacknowledged importance.

Lowry, though not in discussing the creative process, does touch upon the dialectic nature of reality. Addressing a theological issue, he describes sin as "a distorted good." He notes that it is commonplace in contemporary fiction to reveal the bad side of the *good* and the good side of the *bad* in order to sustain ambiguity. Such ambiguity is true to life, Lowry believes; "to look for bad motive in good behavior and to seek noble intention in an evil situation is not just to be effective artists in our work, but to be true to the gospel's estimate of human life."[27] This sounds much like Tillich's statement about the demonic as the perversion of the creative.

In one other place in his book, Lowry touches on an aspect

of the daimonic, even though he does not assign that name to it. In a discussion of sermon preparation, Lowry states that his best sermons began when he was not looking for them. He notes that the harder he tries, the further away the potential sermon seems to be. Conventional wisdom tells us that in order to come up with an "idea" for a sermon, we must study diligently and labor mightily. But such efforts too often yield nothing. However, when studying the Scripture "for its own worth and our own sake," and in reading other material, our minds are free from the "blinders" of conventional wisdom. The result? Frequently, "the serendipitous experience of having a sermon happen when you are not looking."[28]

This discussion is reminiscent of Rollo May's chapter on creativity and the unconscious in his book *The Courage to Create.* May relates an experience he once had in which prolonged efforts to solve a problem he was working on had produced only frustration. Taking a break from his labors in order to "put the whole troublesome business out of my mind," he was suddenly struck "out of the blue" by a solution to the problem. Reflecting on that experience and drawing on similar stories he had heard from other creative persons, May concluded that the unconscious will sometimes break into the conscious with a new insight. A dynamic struggle goes on within the person between what is consciously being thought on the one hand and, on the other, some insight that is struggling to come to light. The breakthrough from the unconscious requires an alternation of intense, conscious work with times of relaxation. May believes that "a *sine qua non* of creativity is the freedom of artists to give all the elements within themselves free play in order to open up the possibility of . . . 'the creative will.' "[29]

Few artists in the modern era have used the term *daimonic* to describe the phenomenon May described. One who did was Rudyard Kipling.

There were his desk, his chair, an enormous wastebasket and his pens—the kind you dip in ink. At right angles to the fireplace was a small sofa. "I lie there," he said with a smile, "and wait for my daemon to tell me what to do."

"Daemon?"

He shrugged. "Intuition. Subconscious. Whatever you want to call it."

"Can you always hear him?"

"No," he said slowly. "Not always. But I learned long ago that it's best to wait until you do. When your daemon says nothing, he usually means no."[30]

As evidenced earlier in this study, Rollo May is one who acknowledges the daimonic in the creative process. Although he takes issue with many of his colleagues who view creativity as "regression in the service of the ego," May concedes that symbol and myth do bring into awareness "infantile, archaic, unconscious longings, dreads and similar psychic content" and that these indeed have a regressive aspect. But, he argues, they also "bring out new meaning, new forms, disclose reality which literally was not present before. . . ."[31] Human creativity, as May sees it, is never free from struggle of the most profound sort. Although he is not speaking of what happens to the preacher when he writes that *creativity occurs in an act of encounter, and is to be understood with this encounter at its center;*[32] I believe those words can be applied directly to the preaching situation. What happens to the preacher in this "encounter"? "Our self-system and sense of identity are literally shaken; the world is not as we experienced it before, and since self and world are always correlated, we are no longer what we were before."[33]

THE PREACHER
AND THE DAIMONIC

In reflecting upon my own experience as a preacher of the gospel, I have become increasingly aware of the daimonic. Certainly for me preparing a sermon has always been a struggle. Part of it is simply the difficulty in putting into words what is in my mind, of moving from "Idea" to "Energy," as Dorothy Sayers put it. But I have discovered that another kind of struggle is even more basic. As I move beyond a critical study of the scriptural text to an existential encounter with it, I find there is set loose in me a variety of responses: memories, anxieties, longings, feelings of insecurity. A natural response is to set such feelings aside in the belief that they are inappropriate to the task of creating a sermon, or in the desire to be spared the internal upheaval that getting in touch with them will involve. Despite these reservations, however, I have frequently been drawn into the struggle and have found the preaching that grows out of it is very often that which calls forth from members of the congregation the most deeply-felt response. Others in the preaching profession have begun to make similar discoveries.

In a discussion of preaching Henri Nouwen defines *dialogue* as "a way of relating to men and women so that they are able to respond to what is said with their own life experience."[1]

> When this dialogue takes place, those who listen will come
> to the recognition of who they really are since the words
> of the preacher will find a sounding board in their own
> hearts and find anchor places in their personal life experi-
> ences. And when they allow his words to come so close as
> to become this flesh and blood, they can say: "What you
> say loudly, I whispered in the dark; what you pronounce
> so clearly, I had some suspicion about; what you put in the
> foreground, I felt in the back of my mind. . . . Yes, I find
> myself in your words because your words come from the
> depths of human experiences and therefore, are not just
> yours but also mine."[2]

Similarly, Charles Rice writes:

> Being human serves the gospel. The more we feel free to
> be ourselves, to be with people, to be free to make mistakes
> and to fail, to celebrate small victories and to cry when the
> tears well up, the more we are likely to serve the Word of
> God. . . . These are the words which describe life as we live
> it and liturgy as we celebrate it, and it is in that range of
> anxiety and joy, of falling ill and getting well, of being born
> and dying, that God addresses to us his Word in Jesus
> Christ. A large part of our vocation as preachers is to let
> ourselves flow more freely in the currents of human life,
> and to keep ourselves open to hear and speak the Word at
> the confluence of our stories and God's Story.[3]

In order for the kind of dialogue Nouwen describes to take
place, and in order for us preachers to "flow more freely in the
currents of human life," as Rice urges, it is necessary for us to
confront the daimonic in ourselves. Without so doing, our
preaching will fail to touch people at the deep places of their
lives, those places where faith and doubt contest, where the
ambiguities of life threaten to overwhelm.

Confronting the Daimonic

For myself, confronting the daimonic happens when I can name my shadow side in the various ways it manifests itself. I must ask, in Jung's language, what are the dark aspects of my personality?

One way I answer that question is by *consciously noting what situations and personal relationships arouse in me strong reactions.* For instance, I may be anticipating a meeting of our church's executive committee. Although I normally do not feel apprehension about these meetings, this time I am nervous and tense. By asking myself why I feel this way, I may discover an unconscious fear that this has triggered my nervousness. It may be that the budget will be under discussion, and, as I think about it, it comes to me that when I look over the proposed budget, the pastoral salary figure jumps out at me. That figure makes me feel guilty because such a large percentage of the budget goes just to pay *me*. An inner voice whispers, "Think of all the *good* the church could do with that money." Memories of my home congregation in which the ministers were unpaid come back to me. I remember the sentiments expressed by those who, at that time, opposed a salaried pastoral system because of the large added expense. I remember the opinion of my father and others that the only *real* work was physical work. White collar workers and professionals had it "soft." They were not really "men." Suddenly, my worth as a male, as a paid professional, as a person, is called into question. No wonder I am feeling tense! My shadow side is at work.

Naming the shadow and wrestling with it can allay my anxiety (or at least help make it manageable), but, more to the point of our inquiry, it can also serve as a powerful ingredient for preaching. I realize that money matters touch people at a very deep level in our culture. A stewardship sermon calls forth in people many responses that preachers never suspect. By naming my own shadow, I am enabled to understand the shadow parts of those who sit in the pews. I can begin to see why sermons about money may leave them feeling anxious, guilty, and defensive. Letting them in on my own struggles with the daimonic will facilitate the dialogue Nouwen speaks of. It can be a way for the redeeming word of God to be released.

To cite another example, the relationship between children and parents is heavy with daimonic overtones. In a variety of ways, the people assembled to hear the preacher have struggled with what it means to be children of their parents. The very words *mother* and *father* evoke reactions in the worshippers that the preacher cannot know. To speak of God as "father" will bring forth a nostalgic, strongly positive response from some. From others, the response may be just as strongly negative. Most likely, however, people who listen to a sermon which refers to parents will respond with highly ambivalent feelings.

One of the best preparations preachers can make in this regard, therefore, is to explore their own feelings about their parents. In my own case, the death of my father from cancer more than a decade ago became a turning point in my preaching. At first, my father's death loomed too large in my psychic history to permit conscious examination. Only gradually was I able to get in touch with some of my feelings about it. Shortly after Dad's death, I had written a short remembrance about him as a way of preserving some of my thoughts for my yet unborn children. Looking at it later, I saw that my remembrance was too sentimental to be accurate. I began to allow myself to relive some of the confrontations between my father and me, to name some of the times when his expressed disappointment in me and his apparent indifference towards me had hurt me deeply. Acknowledging these wounds was a cleansing experience and an enlightening one. What I had thought to be my father's indifference I now realized was part of his own inner struggle — a way of keeping distance so that I could not hurt *him*. I had never allowed myself to imagine the presence of the daimonic in my father; doing so now was a freeing experience that made me able to forgive him and, in some, measure at least, myself.

In my sermons I found myself freer to probe more deeply some of the Scriptures which deal with God as Divine Parent, to be more honest about relationships within families, to speak more openly about my father and how his life affected, and continues to affect, my own. At present, I have begun to explore the ambiguities of my relationship with my mother. This exploration will obviously have implications for my preaching as well.

An illustration of such "implications" appears in the following excerpt, the beginning of a sermon which dealt with the theme of Christian discipleship.

Growing up in Lancaster County, the heart of the Pennsylvania German culture, I knew that tourists came from around the world to stare at the Plain People — mostly the Amish and the Mennonites. Three decades ago, most Brethren in that area also considered themselves "plain people." Our older preachers and deacons still wore the plain-cut, black garb that had once been common among all Dunkers. My mother, like the other women of her age in our congregation, wore her hair long, pinned up, and covered by a prayer veil. As a boy, I gave such matters little thought.

But sometimes our family took car trips. On one such outing — I no longer remember where we went — we chanced to stop at a restaurant. I was in my early teens, an age at which self-consciousness and identity can become painfully acute issues. As we walked through the restaurant, I became aware that people were staring at us, at my mother in particular. I saw a woman lean over and whisper something to her husband.

And in that moment, I was ashamed. Ashamed of my mother and her prayer covering, ashamed of my dad and his job at the feed mill, ashamed of my heritage, of being part of the plain people, ashamed because all of it had conspired to make me and us somehow "different." I took my seat with ears red from embarrassment and sat there in utter misery.

Now before you get upset with that young fellow sitting there in the restaurant, let me assure you that no one could be as hard on him as I have been. Countless times in later years I have been grieved by that boy's shame. I have scolded him, rebuked him, for that moment of betrayal. And I have asked forgiveness — not of my parents, for they never knew of my embarrassment — but forgiveness from myself, first of all, and forgiveness from God. I have been forgiven.[4]

Those who have heard or read this story have reaffirmed my conviction that the kind of "shame" I felt is extremely common among adolescents. Hearing me acknowledge my daimonic in this story framework was a freeing experience for many people. Some breathed audible sighs of relief in telling me that they too had had similar feelings about their parents. This self-awareness opens up the possibility for forgiveness, a particularly crucial issue when adults begin dealing with the difficult matter of aging parents. Seeing parents through the loss of physical strength or the move to a retirement home arouses in adults a vast array of both conscious and unconscious reactions. Preachers who have explored their relationship with their own parents will find that the preaching task has the potential for psychic healing — might we call it "faith healing"? — in the lives of those who listen.

Many life experiences can be explored in much the same way. Why do I get violently angry when someone close to me suffers a severe illness? Why did tears fill my eyes when I saw a white girl and a black girl embrace after a basketball game? What happens inside me when I become nauseous as I watch Oral Roberts on television? Why do I get completely caught up in the emotion of wanting my favorite team to win the World

Series? What was the source of the joy my wife and I felt when we saw for the first time the child we hoped to adopt? Reliving and reflecting on these and other common life experiences can become one of the richest sources for preaching.

It should be noted that while, for me, the daimonic dwells mostly in the realm of feelings, other persons will encounter the daimonic in those parts of their own psyches that have been repressed. People easily in touch with their feelings, for instance, will need to explore the rational, intellectual side of themselves.

A second way to encounter the daimonic is through dreams. In dreams the shadow is free to emerge. Concerns that we have refused to allow into consciousness will appear symbolically in the dream state. During the time I was considering a career change, I had the following dream. At the time I was keeping a journal of my dreams. What follows is an entry from that journal.

> I am in a house that is being refurnished. Dad is there, working to re-do a kind of heating vent. He has done a repair job, but it looks home-made and messy. I tell him it could be done better, but he says, "No, this is all right." Then the two of us are working on an old wall, tearing out the bricks.
>
> Day's Events and Associations
> Two days before, a visit to Chiques Church and Dad's grave. Day before, reading in *The Dream Game* about death and the appearance of deceased people in dreams. On Sunday, had heard Mother say that Dad lived to regret for the rest of his life that he hadn't bought the home farm (taken a big risk).
>
> Dream Characters and Symbols
> Old House—my life
> Heating Vent Patched Up—an example of "how-not-to-do-it"

Dad—himself
Bricks in Wall—my current career status

Dream Message
Dad was never a skillful worker with his hands. He was
"handier" than I am. But, in a sense, I agreed with his
view of himself as a failure. Mother's comment on Sunday about his regret really hit home with me. I disagree
with the one in the dream that a "patched-up" heating
vent is okay. I want to do more than "get by." In the end,
Dad is helping me tear down, dismantle, my present
career position. It's hard work, but it feels right.

Action
Be more deliberate about "dismantling" my status as
pastor. It's a big, important step.

Whether or not my analysis is correct in every particular is
beside the point. Through the effort involved in recalling this
dream and writing down what I believed to be its meaning, I
was able to gain some insight into an important personal event.[5]

The purpose of such careful attention to dreams is not, of
course, to collect material for direct use in sermons. Although
it may occasionally be appropriate to refer to a dream in a
sermon, the real benefit of reflecting on dreams lies in coming
to grips with one's daimonic. The way is thereby opened to
greater understanding of self and of others.

No one who does not know himself can know others. And
in each of us there is another whom we do not know. He
speaks to us in dreams and tells us how differently he sees
us from the way we see ourselves.[6]

This quotation from Jung has particular relevance for preachers. In nearly twenty years of having ministers as fellow-
students, colleagues, and friends, I can recall only rare occasions when the subject of dreams entered a conversation. The
exceptions were those times when someone revealed a dream

that was "funny." The ostensible purpose of sharing the dream was to produce laughter.

In Jungian thought, both dreams and humor are seen as primary revealers of the shadow. Laughter is often provoked by that which we secretly fear or despise in ourselves. Ethnic jokes are primary examples of this phenomenon. When ministers get together, the telling of so-called "off-color" jokes is a common occurrence. The effect of sharing such stories is doubtless therapeutic for people in a profession where expression of the daimonic is strongly discouraged. In much the same way, and with even greater benefit, the sharing of dreams and a serious attempt at helpful interpretation would encourage ministers to gain insights about themselves.

It is not necessary, I believe, to follow a strict Jungian interpretation of dreams. Jung insists, for instance, that the dream figure who represents the shadow, or at least an aspect of the shadow personality, must always be of the same sex as the dreamer because the shadow personifies qualities that could have become part of the ego. Jung also believed that certain dream symbols point to archetypes with a particular meaning. Intensive dream analysis of this kind is not likely to be pursued by many ministers. Nor is it necessary in order for dreams to become a means of self-understanding.

In my own case, a recurring dream related to my work as a preacher has frequently occurred on Saturday nights. In the dream, I am aware that the worship service is about to begin, but something is amiss. In one dream my sermon notes are missing; in another, I am frantic because I have not yet finished my sermon preparation; in still another, the processional hymn has begun and the choir is not lined up to proceed into the sanctuary. By sharing this anxiety dream with fellow clergy, I have learned that they have had similar dreams. Such mutual disclosure provides reassurance that we are not alone in our anxieties and allows us to confess to each other the fears and frustrations related to our common vocation.

Dreams appear frequently in the Bible. Both Old and New Testament writers described dreams and visions and regarded them as legitimate vehicles for divine-human encounter. The writer of Acts records Peter's speech on the day of Pentecost as including a quotation from the prophet Joel. The coming of the Holy Spirit with its unusual manifestations (Acts 2:1–4) was seen by Peter as fulfillment of the Joel prophecy:

> And in the last days it shall be, God declares, that I will pour out my Spirit upon all flesh, and your sons and your daughters shall prophesy, and your young men shall see visions, and your old men shall dream dreams. . . .(Acts 2:17)

The dreams of Jacob, Joseph, Peter, and others, are described in vivid detail in the Bible. In each case, the dreams were an important part of the individual's personal history and thus became important for the faith history of the community.

Yet dreams and visions in the Bible receive scant attention from today's biblical scholars and theologians. In the highly respected four-volume *Interpreter's Dictionary of the Bible*, five full columns are devoted to the entry for "camel"; a single column is given to "dream." The bibliography under this heading refers to one article and two out-of-print books. Small wonder that preachers feel on shaky ground on those rare occasions when they use a scripture about dreams as the text of a sermon. Small wonder too that preachers believe dreams are not worth paying attention to, whether the dreams appear in the pages of holy writ or in their own beds.

A third way I have found of getting in touch with my daimonic is by reading, listening to, and witnessing stories. In some stories, such as *A Wizard of Earthsea*, the daimonic is easily recognizable. But even in realistic fiction or drama, the skill of the storyteller is demonstrated by his or her ability to evoke in the listener an emotive response. This aspect of their art is emphasized by two storytellers in an interview:

M.W. The story and its images enter our experience in a powerful way as we respond with anger, laughter, or stunned silence. That strength of feeling is missed if we intellectualize the stories too soon.

R.S. Right. You really need that emotional response. That is what will make you think about it more and realize that there may be something in the story for you to hang on to.... Stories are so important because you remember them. You remember the characters, what they do and how they feel. That will stay with you, and at different points in your life you will get more food from the same story.[7]

After seeing the film *Ordinary People* and subsequently hearing the positive response to it of friends and parishioners, I reflected on why this particular movie was so powerful. Much of its power, I believe, derives from the fact that in the story of the troubled teenaged son and his parents, the reality of the daimonic is acknowledged. The effects of the son's guilt and insecurity are visible in his attempted suicide and in his loss of control when his friend takes her own life. The effects of the mother's shadow are evident in her inability to reach out in all but perfunctory ways to those she loves. The difference between the son and the mother is that he, with the help of a counselor, is enabled to wrestle with his daimonic. And, in the end, it is the son who experiences the beginning of the healing process.

As I enter into this story, my own insecurities and doubts, my own fear of reaching out to others, are exposed. The story *moves* me; that is, it appeals not simply to my rational side, but to my emotive side. I leave the theater a different person. By reflecting on this experience and by conversation with others who have seen the film, I discover the power that is turned loose when the daimonic is recognized, named, and given voice and form in story.

Unfortunately, many ministers do not think of "reading, listening to, and witnessing stories" as an integral part of preparation for preaching. It is not unusual to hear a member of the clergy state that he or she would *like* to read a novel or take time to see a particular movie but is simply too busy to do so. Stories are regarded as a luxury, as "time off," on par with a round of golf.

Granted, stories do provide a form of escape, a way into a different world. But such trips are not merely a means, a way of taking a break from one's work. Story time is productive time; a story fuels the imagination, opens one to the inner world of both storyteller and story-hearer. It is in this world, says Frederick Buechner, himself both novelist and preacher, that "doubt is pitted against faith, hope against despair, grief against joy."[8] If he is right, then the world of story is a world the preacher must become intimately acquainted with. Far from merely providing a pleasurable respite from the preacher's work, stories are an *essential part* of that work.

The place to begin, of course, is with the stories of the Bible. This subject is addressed more fully in Chapter VI. Here it is worth mentioning that too seldom do preachers allow themselves to be taken into the world of the biblical stories. It is important for the preacher to understand the historical and critical issues related, for example, to the account of the resurrected Christ conversing with his companions on the road to Emmaus (Luke 24:13–35). But it is equally important for the preacher to enter that story, to ask the questions the travelers asked, to feel what they must have felt when, suddenly, "their eyes were opened and they recognized him."

The same kind of willingness to enter the story applies to the reading of fiction, the seeing of a play or film. A story that has the power to seize me, to take me into the world of the imagination, gives, by that very power, a testimony to its importance for understanding the human need for transcendence. Writes Madeleine L'Engle:

> This question of the meaning of being, and dying ... is
> behind the telling of stories around tribal fires at night;
> behind the drawing of animals on the walls of caves; the
> singing of melodies of love in the spring, and of the death
> of green in autumn. It is part of the deepest longing of the
> human psyche, a recurrent ache in the hearts of all God's
> creatures.[9]

Having read the story or seen the play, the preacher must
spend time reflecting upon the story's impact on herself or
himself. Productive questions might be: which character did
I identify with most closely and why? what made me cry or
laugh? what in the story roused fear or anger or loathing in me?
what connections can I make between this story and my own
life story? Such questions become a means, not only of confronting one's daimonic, but also of enabling that confrontation to become a source from which to draw for preaching.

The novel *Sophie's Choice* by William Styron was a story
that helped me confront my daimonic. Reflection on the tragic
story of Sophie became an important part of my preparation for
a sermon on grace, the text of which was the prayer of the tax
collector in Jesus' parable: "God, have mercy on a sinner like
me" (Luke 18:13 TEV). In the sermon itself, I gave a one
paragraph synopsis of Sophie's story — of the choice she is forced
to make in a Nazi concentration camp. Only one of her two
children will be allowed to live, and *she* must decide which
one. Half beside herself with horror, Sophie reaches for her son
and then watches her daughter being pulled away by the
guards. I concluded the sermon:

> After her release from the camp, Sophie cannot come to
> terms with what she has done. She says, "I am so bad; I
> deserve to die." And in the end she takes her own life.
> That is a terrible story; but, my friends, you and I are just
> as capable of such a deed as Sophie was. We all deserve to
> die. And that is why, in the end, the only prayer that can

save us is: "God, have mercy on a sinner like me." For, astounding as it may seem, God accepts sinners.[10]

Releasing the Daimonic in the Preaching Event

After having confronted the daimonic in myself, there remains one final and crucial step, that of translating the fruit of this encounter into the preaching event. The following rubrics are suggested methods for just such translation.

My suggestions are intended to be representative rather than exhaustive. Whatever the method, careful attention must be given to the hoped-for effect. It is not appropriate to the preaching task to aim at manipulating the listeners. Sooner or later they will become aware of such manipulative efforts and will rightly resent them. When the preacher's aim is to have the listeners say, "Yes, this is what I too have felt and known to be true," then the communication process has begun.

For each of the rubrics, I have included examples from my own preaching. I offer them only as illustrations, not as standards by which others should measure their own efforts. The preaching event does not lend itself to copying but grows out of each preacher's personal involvement with the raw materials of human life. The results of that involvement inevitably bear the stamp of the preacher's individuality.

1) Naming and describing common human experiences. It is not difficult for the preacher to speak in generalities about the human condition. In fact, there is great temptation to do just that. Phrases such as "Events in our world can cause us to feel discouraged," or "Sometimes it is hard for us to know what is the right thing to do" roll all too easily from the preacher's tongue. To say, for instance, "Sometimes it is hard to say good-bye," is to state an obvious truth. But such a statement is hardly a revelation to most people. Communication as the kind of dialogue Henri Nouwen commends begins to happen when the listeners can identify moments in their own experience when they have known how hard it is to say good-bye. Naming some "good-bye times" allows listeners to get in touch with their feelings.

> Railroad stations are where people leave home for the first time, and learn the sharp bittersweet taste of the mystery of separation. . . . Railroad stations remind us of other separations: of the school child scrubbed clean and bravely waving good-bye to his tearful mother as he climbs on the school bus for the first time; of the eager young woman kissing her mother and dad good-bye as they prepare to leave her new college dorm room; of tears and smiles and hugs at weddings; of a wasted, dying old man in a wheel chair saying his last good-bye to his daughter waiting to board the airplane. . . .
>
> Maybe you are one of those who says, "I hate good-byes," and you take great pains to avoid them. Part of me feels that way too. But I've come to treasure good-byes as a way of entering into the mystery, the sacrament, of human relationships. I remember Jesus making of his farewell to his disciples a memorial meal, a memory to treasure. And I've discovered that whether separation be temporary or permanent, there is always a kind of dying involved.[11]

There are times when the preacher will want to move beyond merely naming common experiences to describing them. Remembering an actual event can be helpful, but one can also envision a situation. Talking with parishioners who had suffered the anxiety of waiting to learn if they had cancer helped me to create the following scene in a doctor's office. I used the scene as a commentary on an observation about the pain that often accompanies waiting.

> Your physical exam is over, and the doctor comes in, sits down and says softly, "Now I don't want you to worry."

> And your heart jumps to your throat. The doctor continues,
> "I'd like to run another series of tests. By Tuesday we ought
> to know if it's a tumor or something much less serious."
> And you walk out of the office without seeing or hearing
> anything and you wonder how on God's earth you will
> make it till next Tuesday.[12]

Of special help in bringing common human experiences to
life is the use of personal pronouns, particularly the pronoun
"you." In an authoritarian sermon, "you" is used to indict or
to give orders: "you must come to God in full repentance for
your sins." The effect of such usage is to distance the preacher
from the congregation. But in attempting to name and describe
the human condition, the preacher's use of "you" can help to
bridge the gap between speaker and hearer. In the example
cited above, the second person pronoun allowed the congregation to "live" what it means to wait, even if, individually, they
had not actually gone through such a time in their own lives.
What is universal about the scene is the reality of waiting in
anxiety. A scene that depicted a girl anxiously waiting for a
boy to call her for a date could also have made use of "you."
In this latter case, however, half the listeners (the males) would
have been excluded by the second person pronoun. The point
is that many preachers fail to use the pronoun "you" in ways
that invite their listeners to come near.

2) Reporting an actual event. With this rubric, I am not
advocating that the preacher collect a large number of spicy
sermon anecdotes and sprinkle them liberally into the preaching mix. As Richard Jensen notes, such "metaphors of illustration" do not have power in themselves because they are offered
in service of a "point" the preacher is trying to make; "once
the hearers have gotten the point they have graduated from
illustration to information. Having the information fully within
their grasp they may dispense with the metaphor."[13]

The account of an actual event is most likely to touch the listeners if it can stand on its own. If the preacher feels the need to explain how it fits into the point of the sermon, chances are the story will lose much of its impact.

I have also discovered that people have a more pronounced response when they can feel some ownership of the story. Such ownership arises when the story is about an event they themselves participated in or remember or is about someone they know. Drawing on the folk memory of the congregation elicits a strong identification of the listeners with the story. Naturally, before telling a story in which one alludes to or names individuals, it is necessary to get permission from those directly involved. Sensitivity to the feelings of individuals is a must.

The following example is taken from a meditation offered as part of a memorial service for a long-time member of our congregation.

> [Sandy] was active and present here in so many ways . . . checking on the Sunday school classes each week, tapping people on the shoulder to be ushers, lighting the acolyte's taper, fighting his unending (and often unsuccessful) battle to get those of you who sit back on the chairs [at the rear of the sanctuary] up front here where he knew you would be *so* much happier![14]

The second example appeared in a sermon on the theme of holy waste, derived from the account in Mark 14:3–9 of a woman anointing Jesus with costly ointment. The two persons mentioned are members of the congregation.

> I'm reminded of the charming story Vivian B. tells of taking her son Earl Christmas shopping in New York City when he was a youngster. She had given him some money and told him he could use it to buy presents for relatives. The only trouble was, Earl couldn't resist the appeals of the sidewalk Santas. Before they had gone many blocks, his

funds had all found their way into Salvation Army pots. Foolish? Certainly. Wasteful? Maybe. But surely a holy waste—as Vivian's memory of the event eloquently attests.[15]

In both these examples, two elements were present: 1) the congregation's personal acquaintance with the people in the story and 2) the common, day-to-day nature of the events being recounted. If neither element is present, there is little chance that the story will rise above the level of "metaphor of illustration." Stories about events in the lives of famous people— "When Napoleon Bonaparte was preparing his troops for the Battle of Waterloo . . ."—or stories about spectacular events in the lives of common people—"The doctors said he would never walk again, but within three months he was running a mile before breakfast each day"—may illustrate a point in the sermon but have little power to move the listeners.

There are exceptions, of course. I heard a speaker tell about an elderly man in New York who had won five million dollars in the state lottery. Obviously, those in the audience did not know the man who won the money, and the event recounted was a spectacular one. But then the speaker told how a reporter had gone to interview the man a year after he had won the prize and had discovered that very few changes had taken place in the life of this unskilled laborer. He and his wife still lived in the same modest apartment; they had talked about taking a trip to the West Coast but still hadn't gotten around to it. Then the reporter asked: "Do you still buy lottery tickets?" "Oh yes," the man answered, "you've got to have something to hope for." At that point, which was the end of the story, the listeners were brought close to the speaker, to each other, and, I believe, to the God who created within us all that longing which the man in the story expressed so poignantly: "You've got to have something to hope for." His statement was the connecting point, the place where our shared humanity became identifiable.

3) Recounting a story or event with a personal response. Here the emphasis falls on the preacher's own response to the event or story. Translated through the preacher's experience, the story receives additional power. The hearers are drawn primarily not to the story but to the teller's response to it. Their own imaginations are released as they recall similar responses they have had to events or stories that left them changed persons.

As with the previous rubric, there is merit in using events or stories familiar to the listeners. Frequently speakers will ask, "Do you remember what you were doing when you heard Pearl Harbor had been attacked?" (or John Kennedy had been shot?). They may then go on to talk about their own reactions to that public event, knowing that their listeners are actively engaged in the communication process. In much the same way, the preacher can draw on events or stories familiar to most of the congregation and can offer his or her response to them with assurance that the listeners will be eager to compare and contrast the preacher's reactions with their own.

Members of a faith community have in common the stories of Scripture. Preachers spend a great deal of time in sermons talking *about* those stories, saying what the stories "mean," what God's message is, and so on. Much less frequently do preachers divulge what their honest feelings are about the stories. What an opportunity for dialogue is missed! If the preacher is bored by a biblical text, let the preacher say so, and then pursue where the boredom comes from and what its implications are. If the preacher finds the text exciting, let *that* be shared and why. Honest encounter with Scripture can be translated into equally honest encounter with the congregation.

The following example recounts my response to a familiar story from the fourth chapter of the Gospel of John—Jesus' conversation with the Samaritan woman. I began by referring to my previous reactions to the story.

I didn't pay much attention to the narrative, because it seemed obvious that the setting and the story as well as the character of the woman, who is never even named, were of minor importance, almost irrelevant. The woman appeared to serve only as a tool of John the Gospel writer; she seemed to have been included in the story to allow Jesus to make his profound statements. Besides that, she struck me as not very bright, time and time again missing the spiritual point of Jesus' remarks, so that he has to explain patiently to her what he *really* means.

But something surprising happened as I studied the text in preparation for this sermon. For some unknown reason, I gave special attention to the woman's part of the conversation. And when I did, I received a jolt. I saw something I had never seen before: the Samaritan woman isn't a dumb broad at all. She is clever, witty. She banters with Jesus and converses with him as an equal.[16]

I went on to show why such a conversation was unusual given the cultural situation of Jesus' day and then to document the reasons for the "jolt" I had received. The sermon ended with the implications of this "new reading" of the text.

Beyond Scripture, preacher and congregation share knowledge of events that are part of their corporate life, whether in the parish or the larger community. The preacher's response to such events can also provide an opportunity for meaningful communication. In the sermon from which the following quotation is taken, I began by alluding to a news item that had recently appeared in our local paper.

The story told of a man who had died a most untimely death. Or perhaps the opposite is true: the timing was so perfect that its occurrence brought him the national recognition denied him during his lifetime. This man died right in the middle of a wedding service. Now, of course, people have been known to die during weddings before. But this fellow was not a guest at the wedding. He was the groom.

No doubt it was a tragic, extremely upsetting event. What an ironic twist — to have tears of joy transformed into tears of shock and grief. A sad, sad tale without doubt.

Why was it then, that as I read this story in the newspaper, I began to feel a perverse tickle at my funnybone? First, I started to smile. Then I read further and began to snicker. And finally, in spite of my conscience which kept repeating, "But this is a sad, sad tale," I let out a whoop of laughter capable of rattling the coffee cups on our kitchen shelf.[17]

The influence of the daimonic in my reaction to the "sad, sad tale" should be obvious to the reader by now. My sharing of this reaction became an opportunity to reflect on the source of my laughter and to move to a consideration of a biblical story Jesus told about a fool.

Films, TV shows, and best-selling books, all offer stories that become part of our shared experience. In the final example under this rubric, reference is made to a film that had played at local movie theaters not long before. I assumed that some of the congregation had seen it, but I offered a brief synopsis of it for those who had not. I commented that the movie ("Honeysuckle Rose") had not especially appealed to me.

Like I say, hardly the movie of the year. But there was one scene at the end that really got to me, even though the *way* it got to me wasn't what the director had intended. Willie has come home, been reconciled with his family, and all the people in the county have gathered for a barbecue and celebration. The band strikes up some familiar chords and Willie starts singing "Amazing Grace." It becomes a sing-along, with people linking arms and swaying to the easy rhythm. "Amazing grace! how sweet the sound, that saved a wretch like me." Beer bottles are hoisted in a happy salute and smiles reflect the bright glow of the Texas sun. "I once was lost, but now am found, was blind but now I see." I would guess everybody in the movie theater was enjoying this closing scene.

Except me.

I felt uneasy, troubled. It was only a little later that I
figured out why. I was troubled that a beloved hymn had
been reduced to a drinking song. Not because I think "Amazing Grace" should be sung only in churches by long-faced,
strait-laced Christians in their Sunday clothes. It *is* a joyous
song, after all, meant for joyous people. No, what troubled
me was the implication that grace is easy to come by, as easy
as getting together with the gang to hoist a few and sing
the old tunes. The message is clear: grace isn't cause for
amazement any more, only amusement. God isn't even
needed. All it takes is a few good old boys and a keg of
Coors.[18]

4) Telling a personal experience.   Personal stories have been
important in the Christian tradition from Paul's account of his
blindness on the Damascus road to testimonies in frontier tent
meetings. Richard Jensen advocates the use of autobiography
in preaching because listeners can safely listen to someone
else's story. They can laugh or cry or disagree with the teller
because they are not being addressed directly. Jensen finds the
autobiographical method especially helpful when controver-
sial social issues are being considered. He suggests inviting the
hearers into the thought processes the preacher has gone through
on the subject.[19]

For the preacher to tell a personal experience is inevitably
to use the pronoun "I." Traditionally, preachers have been
warned against such personal reference. Certainly the use of
"I" has its dangers, including the danger of making oneself the
center of attention. It is the gospel that must always have this
central position. However, the use of the first person singular
does not necessarily mean the preacher has usurped that position. Preachers whose egos need feeding will find a dozen
different ways to focus attention on them. In most cases, in
fact, the worshippers will resist such efforts.

The people in a worship service have not come to church to find out what "I" see and think and believe. The preacher is *not* that important! But that is only one side of things. The other is that feelings of security, including security with God, can only be experienced if the proclamation happens in a personal fashion. But then we also should say "I"! No word in our language is more personal than "I."[20]

In my own use of autobiography in preaching, I have learned that a special, expectant silence comes over the congregation when I begin to relate a personal experience. The listeners sense that something important is about to be shared, something important, not just about me, but about themselves. They see their own lives mirrored in the event being portrayed. I concur with Sallie TeSelle's statement on autobiography:

> We cannot look at the self directly, for like mercury it squirts away from our sight; but we can evoke the self through a similitude of it, through the metaphor we call autobiography. That is what autobiography is—a likeness or metaphor of the self . . . what we want from other autobiographies is finally self-knowledge.[21]

The following example is taken from an Easter sermon preached on the text in John 9 of the man blind from birth. Immediately preceding my telling of the story of my boyhood experience, the Scripture text was read, concluding with verse 25: "He answered, 'Whether he is a sinner, I do not know; one thing I know, that though I was blind, now I see.' "

> It happened on a Sunday afternoon. On the last Sunday of October. I was twelve years old at the time. We were boys on a Sunday afternoon lark. One of us said, "Let's go explode some old aerosol cans down at the dump. The noise it makes is really neat."

So we went. We were only boys, and knew little of the immutable laws of physics. There was an explosion. I felt a flash of pain. They told me afterwards that I kept screaming, "I can't see. I can't see."

When I awoke in the hospital after the operation, I discovered that my eyes were bandaged shut. And I was afraid and alone in that darkness. Mother and Dad told me the doctor had promised that after a few days the bandages would come off, and that though I would have no sight in one eye, the other was perfectly all right.

I clung to that hope in the long days that followed. And I thirstily drank in every sound around me. "Calling Dr. Miller, Dr. Miller." "Dr. Farmer, please report to O.R." The gentle voices of the nurses were like a caress. The radio became a constant companion—I hummed along with a new song by the Chordettes: "Mr. Sandman, bring me a dream, ba-ba-ba-ba, make him the cutest that I've ever seen."

And then it was remove-the-bandages day. Mother was there. And Dr. Smith—who within 10 more days would be dead of a heart attack—Dr. Smith slowly unwrapped the strips of gauze. "Keep your eyes closed," he said. Then the bandages were off. "Now, Kenneth, slowly open your eyes."

And there *was* light! And my mother's face.

Once I was blind, but now I can see.[22]

In telling the story of my eye injury, I attempted to take the listeners back in time and invite them to live through the events with me. That is one way of relating a personal experience. Another way to do it is to keep oneself and the listeners firmly planted in the present while telling about an event that happened long ago. The effect can perhaps be better labeled "shared memory" than "shared event." The contrast between the two methods can be illustrated by noting the difference between the previous example and the next one, an excerpt from a sermon in which I related a childhood experience of my father reading *Alice in Wonderland* and *Through the Looking Glass* to me. I used this story as a way to approach the parables

of Jesus; specifically, I wanted to take off on the comment by
a biblical scholar that "Jesus advances the parable as an invitation to pass through the looking-glass."[23]

> I'm not sure what I had expected. Perhaps I was too used
> to the "Farmer Jones and His Animals" variety of stories so
> popular at that time—pleasant tales with lots of happiness
> and laughter and never a hint of anything nasty. It didn't
> take me long to discover that the "classics" were different.
> Alice seemed nice enough and so did the white rabbit who
> was introduced on page 2. But *this* rabbit, unlike the ani-
> mals in the storybooks I was familiar with, apparently had
> a sinister side. For when Alice followed him into a hole in
> the ground, she began falling. . . .
> . . . all I could relate to was the terror of falling endlessly
> down that hole. . . . I believe the whole project of father
> reading *Alice* to son came to a halt when we reached the
> Duchess. The picture of her in the book was so ugly, it
> stuck with me for years. So too did the lullaby the Duchess
> sang to her baby. Thirty-three years later, I can still say it
> from memory:
>
> > Speak roughly to your little boy,
> >   And beat him when he sneezes;
> > He only does it to annoy,
> >   Because he knows it teases.
>
> We never finished *Alice in Wonderland.* I read it myself,
> years later, when I could appreciate Lewis Carroll's wonder-
> ful wit and his love of language. *And* when I was old
> enough not to be scared.[24]

5) *Creating a story.*   What I have already said about the relationship of the daimonic to the creative imagination is particularly relevant to creating stories as part of the preaching task.
A story can do what other kinds of address cannot do. A kind
of identification takes place between the listeners and the

characters in the story. Without being consciously aware of it, people hearing the story think and feel their way into the events of the narrative and its characters. The result will often be that the listeners sense the story is meant for them personally. Through this identification with the story, the listeners "infuse the sermon with 'personal content.' " Preachers who tell stories must do so in ways that allow the listeners' experiences to be integrated into the stories. "They must touch that level of existential feelings, of expectation, disappointment, yearning, joy, sadness, and desire; only then do the people in the service hear their own story."[25]

How to touch that level with created stories is a natural question. While there is undeniably an artistic element in creating stories, there are also skills involved, skills that can be learned. In his book *Preaching the Story*, Richard Jensen offers helpful counsel on how to begin this kind of preaching. One of his suggestions is for preachers to start with biblical stories. There is a wealth of material to choose from; any good story will lend itself to retelling. One technique is to tell the story from the viewpoint of a minor character, for example, the story of the prodigal son as the elder brother might have told it. Another method is to take a biblical narrative and recast it into the form of a contemporary story with present-day characters. The drama/sermon which concludes this book has elements of both these approaches.

In *Preaching the Story*, Jensen raises the issue of how open-ended stories should be. As he points out, the great temptation is for the preacher to create a story with an obvious point to it, a clear-cut moral or message. He calls on the preacher as story-teller to firmly resist that temptation. Hans van der Geest takes an opposite view.

> Most listeners are not that subtle in their understanding of stories. It must become quite clear to them what the point is; sophisticated subtleties are for sophisticated ears. The

danger of the narrative sermon is precisely that too much
of what is essential may go unspoken. . . . Here we see the
limits of the narrative; it hardly works or does not work at
all without conceptuality. What is experienced in the story
must be summarized or at least alluded to in clear words
or concepts; otherwise people will feel confused.[26]

In my view, the best stories are those which allow the
hearers to make their own discoveries; they are stories which
spark in the minds and hearts of those who listen a response
that has its own daimonic element. I agree with Fred Craddock
who argues persuasively for inductive preaching that does not
have "the response built into the material." Open-ended preaching, including stories, allows the hearers to reach their own
conclusions. Such freedom is risky, it is "no harmless under-
taking by any means." This kind of preaching is much like a
dream a friend of mine had. He insists that his dream, an
especially vivid one, ended with giant letters spelling out the
words: "TO BE CONTINUED." An open-ended story or sermon
leaves the listeners precisely at that point. "The sermon, not
finished yet, lingers beyond the benediction, with conclusions
to be reached, decisions made, actions taken, and brothers
sought."[27] Story preaching should therefore be open-ended, despite the risks involved. Preaching in story form, as Jensen
rightly observes, is always offered in the context of Christian
worship, within the setting of hymns, prayers, and visual symbols that provide clues for interpretation. The biblical text
offers further interpretation.[28] There is no need, then, to limit
created stories to conventional tales with predictable endings.
Such a limitation would deny the daimonic character of one's
own, and others', faith struggles. It would, in the biblical phrase,
"quench the spirit."

As Jensen says, "The story is the preaching itself."[29] He
supports this assertion with a quotation from fiction writer
Flannery O'Connor.

> People have a habit of saying, "What is the theme of your story?" and they expect you to give them a statement: "The theme of my story is the economic pressure of the machine on the middle class"—or some such absurdity. And when they've got a statement like that, they go off happy and feel it is no longer necessary to read the story.[30]

Time after time the Bible tells a story and then stops. Why should the preacher try to improve on this method?

After creating stories based on biblical narratives, the adventurous and skilled preacher may try a hand at non-biblical creations. The principles discussed above remain the same, and, of course, the aim of the story will still be to proclaim the gospel. The conclusion of one of my own stories follows. The story is told as a boyhood memory by the narrator, who relates the tragedy of two colorful characters, Waab Zink, the town drunk, and Egg-Man Johnny, a mentally retarded man. Both offended the sensibilities of some influential townspeople, and both were later drowned in a flash flood. The text for the story/sermon was Luke 3:1-20, the account of John the Baptist announcing "the wrath to come."

> A joint funeral was held for the two men, and the pastor of the Lutheran Church gave the sermon. He was young, somewhat brash, and used as his text that New Testament phrase about prophets not being honored in their own country. Without mentioning names, he had some harsh words about those who had "conspired" (as he put it) to get Johnny and Waab out of town. Two months later the Lutheran pastor resigned under pressure from certain prominent members of the Church Board.
>
> And if you go to the northeast corner of the town cemetery, you will find two modest headstones standing side by side. They contain the appropriate names and dates, and each carries an inscription taken from the Bible. The first reads: "Let him without sin cast the first stone." The

second: "There was a man sent from God, whose name was John."

To this day, nobody knows who ordered the tomb-stones.[31]

Some Cautions

In the five rubrics I have proposed, there is a gradual intrusion of the first person singular. Obviously, to create a story or a play calls for more of one's own involvement, and energy, than to describe a common human experience. Despite the validity of autobiographical material in preaching, there is a danger that the preacher may begin to use the pulpit to disclose personal intimacies that are inappropriate.

> Preachers must not transform the pulpit into a confessional booth where they vent only their own frustrations, disobedience, and lack of faith. Nor are they to take the pulpit to celebrate the virtue and strength of their own faith. As a listener in the pew, I have problems enough of my own without taking on the preacher's too, and the preacher's strong faith may serve only to complicate my own problems and compound my own guilt.[32]

Admittedly, there is a fine line between what is appropriate and what is inappropriate to share personally in preaching. Feedback from parishioners who can be trusted to be brutally honest can be of great help in this regard. The ultimate test of this or any other method lies in the question: Is the gospel being communicated effectively?

A second caution relates to the discussion in Chapter II. There it was noted that psychologist, theologian, and artist all testified to the destructive possibilities of the daimonic. At this point, there is good reason for recalling that warning. As the daimonic is encountered, first in the preacher's own personal wrestlings, and second in the way those wrestlings become part of the preaching event, significant power will be unleashed.

There is risk. And yet the risk of not encountering the daimonic is even greater. Failure to get in touch with the daimonic will result in preaching that is sterile, relationships that are eroded by hidden conflict, and a church that is stripped of the power it needs to testify to the healing, saving love of God.

As closing, I offer two viewpoints on the matter. The first, from a psychologist, points to the necessity of the preacher's encounter with the daimonic.

> If each of us wrestled with the demonic within we would draw near to each other as fellow sufferers, rather than drawing apart as enemies.[33]

The second comes from a writer of fiction and confirms the inescapable ambiguity of the artist's dilemma, and I would add, the preacher's as well.

> Asher Lev, painter. I looked at my right hand, the hand with which I painted. There was power in that hand. Power to create and destroy. Power to bring pleasure and pain. Power to amuse and horrify. There was in that hand the demonic and the divine at one and the same time. The demonic and the divine were two aspects of the same force. Creation was demonic and divine. Creativity was demonic and divine. Art was demonic and divine. The solitary vision that put new eyes into gouged-out sockets was demonic and divine. I was demonic and divine. Asher Lev, son of Aryeh and Rivkeh Lev, was the child of the Master of the Universe *and* the Other Side.[34]

CHAPTER V

HELPING IT HAPPEN: PRACTICAL CONSIDERATIONS

Every preacher faces the practical necessity of collecting enough material—ideas, words, sentences—to produce a sermon. Confronting my daimonic will inevitably give shape to those ideas, words, and sentences. And yet, there are mundane matters that need attention: how should I prepare myself for the task, what personal resources will help me, what kind of language should I use? This chapter will address such "practical considerations."

Getting Started

The preacher who is willing and able to include his or her daimonic in the preaching task will soon discover that the starting point of any given sermon lies weeks, months, even years, before the first sentence of that sermon is crafted. More will be said on this subject later in this chapter under the subheading, "The Resources of Memory." The relevance of this point here is simply that good preaching requires some work in advance of the actual sitting down to write the sermon.

One of the most productive kinds of preparation consists of drafting a calendar of sermon themes as much as six months in advance. Those preachers who follow the lectionary have the advantage of knowing what the scriptural texts will be on any given day. From time to time I have used the lectionary and found it a helpful discipline. Generally, however, I have felt the lectionary system to be too restrictive. Some of my best sermons sprang from texts never included in the lectionary; the strange story of Judah and Tamar (Genesis 38), for instance, offers a marvelous opportunity for preaching. While the lectionary does include a good many narrative texts from the synoptic Gospels, it gives short shrift to many of the richest Old Testament narratives.

When planning a preaching calendar, I note the special days of the church year that suggest sermon themes. In Advent, obviously, preaching will focus on such themes as preparation, penitence, anticipation, and hope. Other dates on the calendar will be of special significance to the congregation—an anniversary, perhaps, or the celebration of Holy Communion. For the remaining days, I fill in the calendar with possible themes or texts. I may have come across a particular passage of Scripture that strikes me as having creative potential for a sermon. An issue in the life of the congregation demands address. A burning social concern calls for a sermonic response. After preliminary completion of the calendar, I check to see if it is out of balance—not enough pastoral topics possibly, too little attention to life beyond the parish, too much "law" and not enough "gospel." Finally, I try to do some preliminary choosing of scriptural texts for each day. Announcing both the topic and the text in the parish newsletter allows members of the congregation to do their own preparation.

When the calendar has been filled in, I reserve a file folder for each date. Into the appropriate folder go whatever notes, clippings, etc., I have already collected on the theme. In the ensuing weeks I can add more materials as I discover them. When it is time to begin writing the sermon, therefore, I may have on hand a valuable collection of materials. Even more important, *I have invited my daimonic into the preparation process*. My thoughts, feelings, dreams, and memories have had opportunity to be in dialogue with the theme and text. Most preachers recognize the practical necessity of scheduling blocks of uninterrupted time for sermon preparation. Organizing ideas and putting them into words require this discipline. But such private time is even more essential for the part of sermon preparation that often is the most fruitful of all—a period of free flow of ideas, of creative encounter with the text, of allowing the imagination to go where it will. Here I am referring not so much to the use of various biblical translations or commentaries (though these are essential tools) as to the dynamic set in motion by what Eugene Lowry calls "itch" and "scratch."

In his discussion of sermon preparation, Lowry reports that he receives two answers when he asks preachers how they begin. One answer is *finding a theme;* the second answer is *pinpointing a felt need*. But Lowry believes either of the two answers is inadequate by itself. What is needed for a sermon to begin to "happen," Lowry says, is the identification of the intersection point between need and theme. The way to get started, then, is to determine on what one's preliminary thoughts are focused—either on the sensed need or on the theme that is answer to a need. When that focus has been determined, one must begin looking for the other.

> When they intersect in our mind, a sermon idea is born. One might say that any sermon involves both an "itch" and a "scratch" and sermons are born when at least implicitly in the preacher's mind the problematic *itch* intersects a solutional *scratch*—between the particulars of the human predicament and the particularity of the gospel.[1]

That description of a sermon's birth rings true in my own experience. Often the "intersection" that Lowry speaks of takes place unconsciously. But when it takes place, I am finally ready to put pen to paper.

The Uses of a Journal

Many books on preaching advise the preacher to keep a journal of ideas. Some give detailed instructions for cutting out articles, taking notes from books one has read, jotting down illustrations, etc.

No doubt such resources are valuable to some preachers. For me, the efforts to collect materials and file them according to some organized system have produced more frustration than anything else. I may begin work on a sermon about forgiveness, for example, and recall that I had jotted down notes from an article I had read on the subject. Frequently my search for those notes is fruitless. Just as frequently, I find the notes, only to learn they aren't nearly as helpful as I thought they were going to be. What I found stimulating about the article I can no longer remember. And the longer it has been since I read it, the less likely it will be of help in my sermon preparation.

Another kind of journal has been more helpful in my preaching. In it I make dated entries that include a brief synopsis of something I've read or seen or experienced. Then follows my response to the book or event. Sometimes the response is an intellectual one; often it is a description of what my feelings were. The response may, but need not, record an attempt to connect the experience with faith issues.

My purpose in keeping the journal is twofold: first, to record significant moments that might have later use in preaching; and second, to help me bring my daimonic to conscious awareness so I can reap the enlightening, creative benefits that usually accompany this effort. A few entries from my journal can illustrate the process.

(From John Brunner, *From This Day Forward*, a short story — "Fifth Commandment") Old age theme. The old are shut

away in a ghetto—a very pleasant one. They are not told
a new species has been developed after nuclear war. Also
theme of not wanting to know the truth. My feelings—we
all delude ourselves, avoid facing unpleasant truths. We
cooperate with our gentle deceivers.

This brief entry in my journal led to a chancel drama based
on Exodus 20:12, the "fifth commandment." I wrote the drama
six months after reading the story. The drama itself bore no
resemblance to the short story except that it dealt with the
themes of aging and denial of unpleasant truth. But had I not
entered my reactions to the story in my journal, I am virtually
certain the drama would never have been written.

(From Phillip Hallie, *Lest Innocent Blood Be Shed*) The
remarkable, moving story of Le Chambon, a village in south-
ern France, whose people gave sanctuary to refugees from
Nazi oppression. And of the pastor who was the inspiration
for them—Andre Trocmé. The author did a beautiful job
of showing *how* it happened and struggled with the mystery of *why* it happened. In retrospect, as I compare the
goodness, the courage, the caring, and all the rest, of Le
Chambon with the lack of it so many places in Europe and
elsewhere during that time, it seems to me that it is much
easier to explain evil than it is goodness. In my own life,
the same is true. For us, most of what passes for goodness
is duty or boredom or fear of marching to a different drum-
mer. There is very little goodness among us; there is more
evil; but mostly there is "just going along." Going along
with community expectations, or what our parents taught
us or what our fleshly desires lead us into. Maybe the
opposite of evil isn't "goodness" but "holiness." That word
at least takes transcendence into account.
In the Kingdom, not only is evil destroyed, but dullness and
"being good" are transformed into holiness.

From this entry it is easy to see how provocative the book was for me. It is worth emphasizing that what was written down was not the product of careful word choice or thought. Looking back on this entry nearly two years later, I can recapture enough of my initial reactions to remember what the book was about and to renew my interest in some of the theological issues I raised at that time.

> (Event—a day in court, testifying on behalf of a parishioner) What struck me was the sad collection of human beings caught in the net of what society finds unacceptable. What is unacceptable, apparently, is not so much violent or bizarre behavior (hockey game fights are "okay") but rather being poor or of "no-account." The poor, the uneducated who commit an offense are doomed to bear society's anger and retribution.
>
> There were laughs too at some of the testimony given by the bewildered defendants who weren't quite intelligent enough to con the system. What did Jesus mean when he said he came to "free the captives"?

No specific sermon grew out of this experience or the journal entry. But the event itself and my reflective response both have remained with me. In ways I cannot name, they have been part of my preparations for many sermons. Periodic re-reading of this journal entry, and of other entries, triggers thoughts and feelings that enter the mix of my preparations and eventually help create a sermon.

When casting about for a starting point for a sermon, I have found two resources especially helpful; the first is the Scriptures, the second is the entries in my journal. What makes the latter particularly relevant is not so much the events it records, but rather the evidence of the daimonic at work in my personal reflections where I am free to express excitement, anger, sorrow, where I can voice either faith or doubt or some of each,

where I can write down thoughts in the security of knowing
that no one but me will ever read them.

It is this kind of journaling that Frederick Buechner has
commended to his fellow preachers:

> I advise preachers to keep a journal, not of "interesting
> things," but of experiences that they have had, which some-
> how, even if they can't say how, seem either to illumine
> or to be illumined by, religious truth. I tell them to pay
> special attention to any time they find tears in their eyes;
> even if they don't know why the tears are there. Everybody
> has these experiences, if not once a day, at least once a
> week. My message to preachers is: "Wake up, be alive,
> listen to what's happening in your own life!"[2]

The Resources of Memory

The subject of keeping a journal raises the issue of memory
as a resource for preaching. Human memory, as those who
have studied it well know, is a complex matter. In the first
place, memory can not produce literal recordings of the past.
Memory is selective; it reconstructs the past to fit the stories
we keep to help us know who we are and how we got that way.
Rather than thinking of memories as mental photographs of
the past, we do better to think in terms of impressionist paint-
ings. Through memory, our past experiences are returned to
us more nearly as portraits painted by our psyches.

The application of memory to preaching is found in the
centrality of memory in the Bible. One way of understanding
the Scriptures is as the collected memories of the faith community. Remembering played a significant role in ancient Israel.
The people of Israel believed that bringing an event or a person
to memory was to make the event or person a present reality.
In the book of Deuteronomy, Moses is portrayed as constantly
telling the people to remember their experience as slaves in
Egypt and later as wanderers.

You shall remember that you were a slave in the land of
Egypt, and the Lord your God redeemed you ... (Deut.
15:15)
And you shall remember all the way which the Lord your
God has led you these forty years in the wilderness, that he
might humble you, testing you to know what was in your
heart ... (Deut. 8:2)

One of the most important roles of the clergy in our day is
that of carrying on the legacy of Moses by helping the faithful
to remember. The celebration of the Eucharist is the corner-
stone: "Do this in remembrance of me." But preaching is also
an indispensable tool of memory. By drawing on the memory
documents of Scripture for sermon texts, the preacher keeps
before the people the importance of the received tradition. By
thus honoring memory and its relationship to faith, the preacher
validates the important place of memory in the lives of each
member of the listening congregation.

The most meaningful way I have found for helping this to
happen is by drawing on my own memories and incorporating
them into sermons. In my early years as a pastor, I did so
somewhat reluctantly and apologetically. I believed it was pre-
sumptuous to talk about myself when what the congregation
hungered for was God's word for their own lives. But what I
discovered was an incredibly positive response to my use of
personal memory. I believe this response meant that my use
of memory had awakened the memories of the listeners. For
the most part, my remembrances were of simple, everyday
events, the kind of things that nearly all people have experienced. An example is a story I told about being afraid of the
dark.

One of my chores as a youngster was disposing of the
potato peelings and other wastes after the evening meal.
(We were less genteel in those days; Dad simply said: "Son,
take out the garbage.") In summertime, this chore present-

ed no problems. But it was a different story during the winter months. My route called for a trip to the end of our long backyard sidewalk, up a small bank, down a short gravel path, through the gate in the chicken yard fence, along another path, across a small creek, and a short way beyond it to the garbage heap. In all, it was a distance of about fifty yards, but on dark winter nights, it seemed like miles.

I knew, logically, that there was nothing to harm me out there. We lived out in the country; no danger from criminals, no wild animals roamed our backyard. And so I would begin walking down the pavement. Soon I was jogging. Then I was running. Many a night I stopped well short of the creek and wildly flung the contents of the garbage dish into the blackness, turned tail, and ran for my life. My *mind* told me: "nothing to be afraid of," but my *imagination* pictured unnameable creatures nipping at my heels. It was only in later years that I discovered my imagination had been right all along.[3]

A word of warning is in order at this point. Memory can become an easy avenue into nostalgia. When indulged in to excess, nostalgia is dangerous because it prevents us from taking the past seriously and seduces us into supposing the future is too terrifying to contemplate. Remembering is a different thing. It neither trivializes nor falsely glamorizes the past.

In the introduction to his autobiography, Frederick Buechner admits that one of the appeals of memory is nostalgia with its strong backward pull to an imagined time of innocence. He goes on to say:

But even if it were possible to return to those days, I would never choose to. . . . It is mainly for some clue to where I am going that I search through where I have been. . . . I listen back to a time when nothing was much farther from my thoughts than God for an echo of the gutterals and sibilants and vowellessness by which I believe that even then God was addressing me out of my life as he addresses us all. . . .

My assumption is that the story of any one of us is in some measure the story of us all.[4]

Buechner's words help explain why the use of memory in a sermon can become such a powerful means of bringing preacher and hearers together in openness to God's Spirit.

In order to have memory become a resource for my preaching, I must use it frequently. One way of doing so is to take a trip to the attic to dig out old notebooks, high school yearbooks, photo albums, etc. Time is well spent just allowing myself to free associate. I am continually amazed how one memory will spark another — a remembrance of a person or an event I had not thought about for years. Another way of training memory is to memorize (in some cases, rememorize) favorite poems or passages of Scripture. Conversation with older people who draw on their memories is another helpful tool. I begin to discover that one of the richest resources for speaking humanly, for being personal in a way that invites the listeners to come close, is the memories tucked away in my unconscious.

"If I am to be a storyteller I must have a trained memory. No memory, no story."[5] That sentiment expressed by Madeleine L'Engle holds equally true for the preacher. Memory, especially childhood memory, strips away our pretensions and pride, woos us to a state of being in which it is easy to "become like children" (Matt. 18:3). And maybe, by God's grace, to enable us and our listeners to enter the Kingdom — even if only for a glimpse.

An Argument for the Concrete

Flannery O'Connor, a novelist and short story writer who died in 1964, did not live long enough to publish many books. Yet the importance of her contribution to American fiction is universally recognized in literary quarters. As a Roman Catholic, O'Connor was particularly distressed by what she called "the Manichean spirit" of writers who identified themselves as Christians. What she meant by that phrase was the tendency she saw in many writers of fiction to concern themselves with "unfleshed ideas and emotions." Just as the Manicheans separated matter and spirit, so many writers, said O'Connor, "will put down one intensely emotional or keenly perceptive sentence after the other, and the result will be complete dullness."[6]

Unfortunately, O'Connor's judgment would apply with equal validity to much contemporary preaching. Sermons too easily get filled up with generalities, abstract statements, sociological observations, theological propositions. All — or at least most — of them may be true enough, but they fail to engage the listeners.

"We have a desperate need to reassure ourselves that we are indeed of worth." Few in the listening congregation will argue with such a statement, but what does it mean translated into their own lives? Unless such a statement is followed by specific reference to a person or to an event, the truth it contains will remain a lifeless abstraction.

"Perhaps the greatest task before us is opening ourselves and our congregation to the will of God." Such a statement may or may not be true — who is to say, after all, what constitutes "greatest"? It obviously was meant to be an important statement in the context of the sermon in which it appeared. But it lacks concreteness. "Greatest task," "opening ourselves," "will of God" are phrases that preachers resort to all too often. Such phrases sound good, feel right . . . and say nothing the listeners can get their hands on.

I came to recognize this tendency in my own preaching when I looked back at some of the funeral meditations I had preached. I was chagrined to come across a sentence like this: "Those of us who have been loved by someone have received life's greatest blessing." But I failed to say what it meant to those who were loved by *this* person. What *particular* blessing was it, and what particular pain went along with it? On another occasion I had said: "All of us have successes and failures in life, and John had his share of both." Again, an undeniably true statement. But again, a lifeless generalization (though I had at least used the person's name). But what *were* some of those successes and failures? What made this individual a unique human being, an unrepeatable character in "the great story and plot of all time and space . . . [created by] the great dramatist and storyteller, God himself"?[7] Death in general is a philosopher's theme. Death to this person in particular is a life-changing experience.

The Bible is filled with specific, concrete language. It is remarkably free of concepts and theological abstractions. Words like "atonement," "justification by faith," or "eschatalogical apocalypticism," are either rare or absent altogether. True to the Hebrew understanding of reality, the Bible concentrates on people and places and events.

The language of preaching should also be concrete. It should be *incarnational* language. Among other things the New Testament witnesses to is that the incarnation of God in Jesus led to the particular death of a particular man on a particular cross. There is nothing esoteric or spiritualized in the Gospels' account of the events leading up to and including the crucifixion. Concrete details abound: feet washed and then wiped with a towel, a condemned man's robe gambled for by soldiers, a sword thrust into a side and "came there out blood and water" (John 19:34 KJV).[8]

One way to work towards more concrete language is to give close attention to the nouns and verbs used in sermons. An abundance of polysyllabic nouns usually points to abstract, fuzzy language. As much as possible, nouns should be picture words rather than idea words. "Material possessions" probably means "money." Why not say so? Action verbs are better than forms of the verb to "to be." Active voice is better than passive voice. Preachers should keep on the lookout for stock phrases that constantly appear in their sermons. One of my favorites is "the Kingdom of God." *I* know what I mean by the phrase, so I assume my listeners do too. Most of them do not.

Fred Craddock reminds preachers that they are seeking to communicate with people whose experiences are concrete. Yet, he finds, a fear of concreteness seems to haunt the pulpit. Why cannot preachers remember that a farmer deals not with "calf-hood" but with a calf? "The minister says 'all men are mortal' and meets drowsy agreement; he announces that 'Mr. Brown's son is dying' and the church becomes the church.'"⁹

One of the benefits of encounter with the daimonic is the resulting push towards concreteness. If I have been willing to allow my daimonic to emerge through reflections about people and events, through dreams, through stories, the chances are good that my preaching will draw on them and will, of necessity, require the use of concrete language.

Finally, the whole matter of authority in preaching bears a closer relationship to concreteness of language than has generally been recognized. Flannery O'Connor was arguing for the importance of concrete language by fiction writers in the following quotation, but the application of her words to preachers is profound . . . and startling.

> No reader who doesn't actually experience, who isn't made to feel, the story is going to believe anything the fiction writer merely tells him. The first and most obvious characteristic of fiction is that it deals with reality through what can be seen, heard, smelt, tasted, and touched.¹⁰

The preacher will hear in those words a challenge to concrete language, not merely as a means of improving the quality of a sermon, but as a way of being faithful to a central affirmation of Christian faith:

That which was from the beginning, which we have heard, which we have seen with our eyes, which we have looked upon, and our hands have handled, of the Word of life (1 John 1:1).

CHAPTER VI

WRESTLING JACOB:
AN ENCOUNTER
WITH THE DAIMONIC

The bulk of this final chapter is devoted to a detailed critical study of a particular Old Testament text and to the drama/ sermon which grew out of my own "wrestling" with the text. Readers may register some surprise at the number of pages given to critical study and textual commentary in light of the emphasis on the daimonic that has been so integral to this book. But acknowledgment of the importance of the daimonic in preaching *in no way* obviates the necessity for rigorous application of analytical tools, the use of which was learned in seminary courses. On the contrary, biblical criticism is absolutely essential as a prerequisite for authoritative preaching. Without it, my daimonic may well lead me into dubious uses of Scripture, such as employing it to justify my own biases or allegorizing it to lend credence to a specific ax I have to grind. Serious critical study assures that the text is seen and understood in its peculiar historical setting; its "message" will be recognized as an entity that cannot be lifted out of its setting and transferred whole to our own time. This recognition is necessary to preserve the integrity of the biblical word.

There are other benefits as well. Biblical criticism sets the words of the text free from preconceived notions of its truth imposed by doctrinal dictums. Critical study helps us understand how the text may have undergone changes as new generations sought to understand God's word in their own time. We are freed to undertake the same kind of understanding. I agree with Walter Wink's assessment of the value of critical study when he observes that "biblical criticism can liberate the intellect to radical truthfulness, personal integrity, and rational responsibility."[1]

The text chosen for study is an Old Testament narrative in which one of the main characters is a shadowy figure identified as "a man." In the story this personage acts in ways that resemble the behavior of Old Testament daimons (see Chapter I)—this, despite the fact that Jacob eventually identifies his assailant as God. The Hebrew word *elohim* contains sufficient ambiguity to allow for the creative tension that makes the story so compelling; i.e., who *is* Jacob's adversary and does he really want to destroy Jacob?

This divine/daimonic ambiguity which runs throughout much of the Old Testament seems to disappear in the New Testament, where, as we saw in Chapter I, the existence of demons as evil spirits is commonly accepted. Jesus understood part of his task as asserting the power of God against the power of Satan (see, for example, Mark 1:23-27 and John 12:31). The casting out of demons and evil spirits was a primary part of his healing ministry. Yet those who observed Jesus suspected that he himself was possessed by an unclean spirit. A remarkable section of Mark's Gospel states that even his friends held this suspicion: " ... when his friends heard it, they went out to seize him, for they said, 'He is beside himself' " (Mark 3:21). The verses that follow tell of the scribes who attributed Jesus' powers of exorcism to his being "possessed by Beelzebul"; "by the prince of demons he casts out demons" (Mark 3:22). Jesus denied their charge:

If Satan has risen up against himself and is divided, he cannot stand, but is coming to an end. But no one can enter a strong man's house and plunder his goods, unless he first binds the strong man; then indeed he may plunder his house. (Mark 3:26–27)

Whether the plunderer in this analogy is Satan or is Jesus himself entering Satan's house is not clear. What *is* clear, however, is that Jesus, regardless of what his exact understanding of Satan might have been, was willing to confront the demons face to face, to meet them on their own turf, to call them by name. At the outset of his ministry, he went to the wilderness "to be tempted by the Devil" (Matt. 4:1). Jesus did not deny the demons their right to exist. What he *did* deny was their right of *possession*. The solution was not simply to drive out the demons. As this cryptic story, recorded in Matt. 12:43–45, suggests, Jesus understood that the expelling of an evil spirit leaves a person vulnerable to subsequent possession. What was needed was the transforming of the demon into a force for good.

Some modern interpreters go so far as to attribute to Jesus certain Jungian insights about the shadow side of the personality. John A. Sanford interprets Jesus' saying, "Make friends quickly with your accuser" (Matt. 5:25), as a psychological insight in which the accuser with whom we must come to terms is the shadow personality. Sanford summarizes the message of Jesus by stating:

What Jesus is urging, then, is that our lives and personalities are to be brought to completeness. . . . This will necessarily involve recognition of the Shadow and the acceptance of this part of ourselves as an inevitable part of our totality. The solution to the shadow problem that Jesus suggests, then, involves the growth of psychological consciousness and spiritual maturity by the recognition of our dark side as well as our light side.[2]

Such a reading of what Jesus was about ignores the historical milieu in which Jesus lived. It also conveniently ignores the many references to Jesus casting out demons.

Rather than turning Jesus into an apologist for twentieth century psychological insights, we do better to recognize that in Jesus' day the existence of both good and evil spirits was readily acknowledged. We are on safer ground when we note that Jesus chose among his disciples two men in whom spirits battled each other. One, of course, was Judas (see John 6:70–71). The result of Judas' inner struggle was tragic. Peter, on the other hand, emerged from his inward struggles a man of integrity and strength. Luke 22:31–32 records the words of Jesus to Simon Peter.

> Simon, Simon, behold, Satan demanded to have you, that he might sift you like wheat, but I have prayed for you that your faith may not fail; and when you have turned again, strengthen your brethren.

These moving words are evidence that Jesus recognized both the creative and the destructive possibilities of Peter's spiritual struggle. In time it could be said of Peter that he was filled with the Holy Spirit (Acts 4:8).

The New Testament, then, while it highlights the threat of the demonic to humankind, can actually be helpful to me as a preacher as I explore my own daimonic. I learn that there is risk involved, but a risk that must be taken. I am helped by the counsel of the New Testament writer who urged, "Beloved, do not believe every spirit, but test the spirits to see whether they are of God" (1 John 4:1). The daimonic must be indeed tested, as I meet my shadow side, as I find myself in relationships with others, and finally, as I wrestle with the scriptural text and embark on the exciting venture of creating a sermon.

Exegesis of Genesis 32:22-32

Definition of the Unit

The narrative of Jacob's wrestling match with his nocturnal adversary is set in the larger context of Jacob going to meet his brother Esau. In Gen. 32:3-8, the narrator says that Jacob, in returning to his homeland, understood that the confrontation with his brother, whom he had cheated of his birthright many years before, was fraught with danger. When he hears that Esau is on his way to meet him, Jacob is "greatly afraid and distressed" (32:7). He prays to Yahweh to deliver him from his brother's vengeance (32:1-12) and then, perhaps in an effort to hedge his bets, tries another approach: he prepares lavish gifts for Esau. "For he thought, 'I may appease him with the present that goes before me, and afterwards I shall see his face; perhaps he will accept me' "(32:20).

At this point the narrative is interrupted by the encounter on the riverbank. Verses 22-23 shift attention away from the Jacob-Esau meeting and serve as an introduction to Jacob's critical struggle with his assailant. Jacob takes his family and all his possessions across the ford of the Jabbok. Then, says the text, "Jacob was left alone. . . ." (24a). What follows is Jacob's struggle with the "man" who attacks him in the darkness. The struggle is resolved in verse 29 with the adversary granting Jacob the requested blessing. The final three verses of the unit (30-32) offer an etiology of the name *Penuel* and the custom of not eating the sinew of the hip.

Chapter 33, verse 1, resumes the story of the Jacob-Esau confrontation. It could follow immediately after 32:31 and make a smoothly flowing narrative. The "therefore" which begins verse 32 is similar to the "therefore" in the etiology of 26:33, a verse which also concludes a literary unit.

Supporting the contention that 32:22-32 is a unit are the number of contemporary English translations which begin a new paragraph with 32:22 and conclude with verse 32. Among them are the Revised Standard Version, the Jerusalem Bible, The New English Bible, New American Standard Bible, and Today's English Version. Modern commentators also treat 32:22–32 as a separate unit. Vawter sees it as a redactional section formed from a combination of earlier source materials. He chooses to characterize these verses as "not of a piece with the rest of the Jacob narrative."[3] Von Rad defines the unit as consisting of verses 22–32, though, unlike Vawter, he believes Jacob's wrestling match is integrally related to the Jacob-Esau meeting.[4]

Text and Translation

An important part of the narrative hinges on the identity of the one who wrestled with Jacob. In 32:24 Jacob's adversary is "a man." Vawter contends that *someone* might be a better rendering of the Hebrew *ish*.[5] Speiser translates it as "some man."[6] Later it is discovered that Jacob's opponent (v. 29) has been God, or better, *gods*. The Hebrew word is *elohim*. Hosea, in his reference to the story, says that Jacob "in his manhood . . . strove with God. He strove with the angel. . . ." (Hos. 12:2b–3a).

The change of names is also critical to an understanding of the text. The Oxford Annotated Revised Standard Version, in a footnote to verse 28, gives the literal translation of *Israel* as "He who strives with God" or "God strives." Speiser appeals to S. R. Driver's etymological translation: "May El persevere."[7] The text itself offers as the explanation for the name change the assailant's word to Jacob: " 'Your name shall no more be called Jacob, but Israel, for you have striven with God and with men, and have prevailed' " (32–28).

A final translation problem is the place name that appears twice, in verses 30 and 31. The first spelling is "Peniel"; the second, "Penuel." Commentators agree that the variant in spelling does not signify anything more than two coexisting forms of the traditional name Jacob gave to the place of his momen-

tous encounter. Literally, Peniel means *the face of El.* Von Rad
sees Penuel as a pun on the word for *face,* particularly in
connection with the five-fold usage of "face" (*pānīm*) in 32:20–
21.⁸ The theme is picked up again in 33:10 where Jacob tells
Esau that seeing Esau's face " 'is like seeing the face of God.' "

Analysis of the Unit

Structure

The episode of Jacob at the Jabbok fits into the most common
of all literary plot structures: tension — conflict — resolution.
What makes this structure of special interest, of course, is the
theophany which is used as transition from the foregoing part
of the narrative and as an introduction to a new episode. The
storyteller is preparing the listeners for something significant
as the minor characters are shuffled off-stage in verses 22 and
23. Obviously a momentous event is in the making, one that
requires Jacob to be completely without aid from family, servants, or even material possessions, including weapons. "Everything that he had," the text says, was sent across the stream.
Then come the stark, bone-chilling words, "And Jacob was
left alone" (24a). Anyone who has been in a strange place, at
night, all alone, will feel the terror of the unknown that Jacob
must have experienced. Tension has mounted to the breaking
point.

Then suddenly the tension is broken by the attack of Jacob's
assailant. Physical combat follows. But finally, Jacob's opponent, seeing that physical prowess will not overcome Jacob,
attempts to negotiate: " 'Let me go, for the day is breaking' "
(v. 26). The conflict then becomes a verbal one through verse
29, and ends with the narrator's words: "And there he blessed
him."

The episode does not conclude immediately, however. Jacob
christens the place of the struggle with the name *Peniel.* Then
as the sun rises, he limps away from the place; and the narrator

offers an explanation for an Israelite cultic practice by connecting it with Jacob's limp and how he received it.

In this episode a master storyteller is at work. Drawing from various sources, he has crafted a chilling tale in which the folk-hero meets and overcomes in hand-to-hand combat a divine or semidivine adversary. The story has an introduction, a body, and a conclusion. It is the kind of story that has thrilled listeners for thousands of years: the hero is in trouble; the outcome is in doubt till the very end; the hero emerges victorious, his reputation more glorious than before.

In outline, the structure is as follows:

I. Introduction (Creation of Tension)   22:24a
  A. Setting of the Stage (Jacob's family and
     possessions are sent across the river)   22–23
  B. Final Preparation for the Conflict
     (Jacob is left alone)   24a
II. Conflict (Theophany)   24b–29
  A. Wrestling Match   24b–25
    1. A "man" wrestles with Jacob   24b
    2. Jacob's thigh is put out of joint   25
  B. Verbal Struggle   26–29
    1. Request for release and Jacob's refusal   26
    2. Request for name and Jacob's answer   27
    3. Renaming of Jacob (etymological etiology)   28
    4. Jacob's request for adversary's name
      and refusal   29a
    5. Bestowal of blessing   29b
III. Resolution and Conclusion   30–31
  A. Jacob names the place (etymological etiology)   30
  B. Conclusion   31
IV. Afterword (Cultic Etiology)   32

Genre

This passage is obviously narrative; it contains setting, plot, and characterization.

Otto Eissfeldt, whose work rested on the prior findings of Gunkel, distinguished six types of poetic narrative: myths, fairy tales, sagas, legends, anecdotes, and tales. The latter two have entertainment as their primary purpose and do not deal with history.[9] Myths and fairy tales both deal with actions in the realm of the supernatural; myths with actions among the gods, fairy tales with supernatural and magical events in human affairs. Sagas and legends differ from these two in that they are attached to specific persons, places, and times, even though they include elements of the miraculous or marvelous. In legends, unlike sagas, the specific places or persons in the story are directly involved with religious meaning.[10]

The Jacob at the Jabbok narrative fits into the category of either saga or legend. By Eissfeldt's definition, the final form of the narrative can best be called a legend, for it clearly contains a religious element. More than a tribal or national saga, it expresses a relationship between God and the patriarch. The other religious reference is found in the etiology of the cultus, the practice of not eating the sinew of the hip.

Stages in Formation

The literary history of the passage, as with so many Old Testament passages, can only be conjectured.[11] However, a look at the text indicates that the story obviously underwent change and adaptation before it reached its final form.

Certain discrepancies in the text point to this process. In verse 22 the text reads: "Now he arose that same night and took his two wives . . . and crossed the ford of the Jabbok." In verse 23 the text reads: "And he took and sent them across the stream." There are thus two crossings of the stream, with no explanation. Another discrepancy is found in verse 26, where the adversary, who has dislocated Jacob's thigh, and thus apparently gained the upper hand, pleads for release.

In attempting to explain such discrepancies, scholars have posited two basic explanations. Either the passage was created from a variety of sources with many redactions or the passage can be attributed primarily to a single author, namely, the Yahwist.

Among those who hold to a hypothesis that the passage underwent an extensive series of redactions are C. A. Simpson, H. Seebass, H. Gunkel, and H. Holzinger. All employ a form of the documentary hypothesis and attribute parts of the passage to J1, J2, E, and JE.[12]

Opposed to this view is an approach which regards the passage as a unity and credits the Yahwist with authorship. S. R. Driver, W. Eichrodt, O. Eissfeldt, and G. von Rad, among others, subscribe to this view. As they see it, the passage has very little literary history but contains a wealth of traditional history. Discrepancies in the final form of the narrative are accounted for by efforts to fit this episode into the larger narrative unit and other legitimate literary concerns.

The kernel of the story is found in the ancient myth of the rivergods, who demanded tribute such as payment or sacrifice before they would allow humans to cross. Ancient heroes frequently engaged in combat with these deities on riverbanks.[13] Further, it was quite common for gods to insist upon leaving the scene before daybreak.[14]

Another important element in the story is the naming. Ancient belief attributed great power to the giving and receiving of names and to the invoking of names for incantational purposes. To know the name of a person or a god was to wield power over him, to control his identity, or to take that identity for oneself.[15]

Gaster speculates that in an earlier version of the story, Jacob waited alone purposely so he could combat the rivergod and obtain a blessing.[16] Robert Martin-Achard prefers to think that the Israelites took over the story of a legendary hero vanquishing the rivergod and substituted Jacob as the hero. When the Yahwist gave final form to the legend, he took care that the outcome was not clearcut. It was unthinkable that Jacob should

overcome Yahweh. The proper name of Israel's God was care-
fully avoided.

> Jacob must neither win nor be defeated in too obvious a
> manner. He will finally have to release his hold, but his
> adversary will respect his resistance. . . . The Yahwist sug-
> gests that the last word remains with divine grace by em-
> phasizing that, contrary to every expectation, Jacob is
> discharged alive from his encounter with God.[17]

Purpose

Within the context of the entire Jacob narrative, this unit
functions as a turning point. In terms of Jacob's anticipated
meeting with Esau, the tension of that potential conflict has
had its edge dulled considerably. When the narrative returns
to that encounter (33:1–15), the terror Jacob had earlier felt in
32:7–20 seems markedly reduced. Although Jacob goes to meet
Esau with great show of humility (33:3), there is nothing to
suggest the fear and trembling of the previous night. Jacob's
comment to his brother in 33:10 (" 'to see your face is like
seeing the face of God . . .' ") suggests that Jacob's struggle with
his opponent on the riverbank has given him a new perspective on things. When one has wrestled with God himself, how
can one be terrified at the thought of conflict with mortals?

More importantly, the unit is a turning point in terms of
Israel's theological understanding of its reason for being. The
patriarch Jacob, in his encounter with God, receives the divine
blessing. From now on, he is more than a folk-hero about
whom interesting tales are told; he is, in fact, the prototype of
the people who will later bear his divinely-given name, Israel.

> In its final form in the book of Genesis, it [this story] at least
> points to the fact that Jacob is entering a new land, the land
> of promise. He is to receive the promise not primarily by
> his own astuteness, but by the gift of God. . . . [Jacob] ac-
> quires the name ISRAEL and enters on the new life which

God has prepared for him — the ancestor of his people Israel.[18]

The ending of the unit, however, is not free from ambiguity. Jacob may have "striven with God . . . and prevailed," but he bears the marks of that striving, that is, he is lamed. Jacob's new life and new name have been won at a heavy price. He will forever be maimed. But there is a purpose to it. It will be an ongoing reminder that one enters into combat with God at no small risk. Nor can one expect to emerge unscathed. And yet, Jacob's lameness is a symbolic badge of courage. Rather than a cause for shame or embarrassment, it is transformed into an emblem of honor. Verse 32, which offers a cultic etiology, is an obvious addendum to the story. Sarna suggests that an ancient and well-known Israelite practice of not eating the sinew of the hip is here given an important theological interpretation. In many ancient cultures, the thigh region held special significance because of its nearness to the reproductive organs and was considered to have sacral meaning (see Gen. 24:9). But here such origins of a cultic practice are ignored in favor of an explanation rooted in the history of Israel, so that the dietary taboo commemorates an event of "epochal importance."[19]

Whatever the origins of the story of Jacob at the Jabbok, its final form declares that Jacob has been delivered. But the deliverance is not the one he had prayed for (32:11) — it is far greater. He is no longer Jacob, the Supplanter, but Israel. And Israel, as the people who bear their ancestor's name, will indeed strive with God. Their entire history will be the record of this striving. They too will bear the marks of the struggle. They will frequently encounter the adversary in the darkness of captivity, seige, and exile. But out of this struggle will come a tested and seasoned people, a people whose experience with God equips them uniquely to proclaim his name and will to all people. Their existence as a people becomes evidence of

God's deliverance, of God's intention to redeem, save, and set free.

Commentary

What I offer here is not a commentary in the traditional sense. Instead, I will describe several different methods of approaching a biblical text and then present my response to the story of Jacob at the Jabbok by using one of those methods. Of necessity, there will be a pronounced personal flavor to my reflections.

First, then, a word about the choosing of Gen. 32:22–32 as the text for the drama/sermon that follows. I have already stated that "*wrestling* is indeed the proper word to describe the preacher's personal, existential encounter with the biblical text."[20] It is not so strange, then, that to illustrate how the daimonic can become part of the preaching event I should settle upon the well-known story of Jacob's wrestling match with God. But there were other reasons for this choice. They did not occur to me until after the choice was made, but I suspect they played an unconscious role in it.

My brother, twelve years older than I, was a member of his high school wrestling team. Some of my earliest and best memories of our relationship are of my brother practicing his newly learned wrestling holds on me: half-nelson, roll, cradle. In those encounters we experienced an intimacy of touching and holding that was played out in the context of physical struggle. The paradoxical nature of our relationship—rival/comrade— was symbolized beautifully as we grappled in mock combat. When I reached high school age myself, I participated in only one varsity sport: wrestling.

There is another pull towards the story of Jacob that doubtless influenced me. My paternal grandfather, who died before I was born, was known to me only by the stories told about him by my father and his kin. In a few yellowed photographs, Grandpa Gibble, the patriarch, looked out at me from a stern visage with a long white beard. His name was Israel.

I wrestled again with my brother last week,
First time since I was twelve and Grandma stopped us:
"She won't even let us fight!" we yelled, embracing,
But she said talking was nicer.
Wrestling feels a lot like making love.
Why did Jacob wrestle with God, why did the others talk?
God surely enjoyed that all-night fling with Jacob:
Told him he'd won,
Renamed him and us the Godwrestler,
Even left him a limp to be sure he'd remember it all.
But ever since, we've talked.
Did something peculiar happen that night?
Did somebody say next day we shouldn't wrestle? Who?

We should wrestle again with our Comrade sometime soon.
Wrestling feels a lot like making love.

But Esau struggled to his feet from his own Wrestle,
And gasped across the river to his brother:
It also
Feels
A lot
Like
Making
War.[21]

This poem by Arthur I. Waskow bears evidence of the struggle that ought to typify the preaching event. The poem can stand on its own, but in the book in which it appears, it is prelude to a chapter in which the author wrestles with the story of Jacob and his adversary. The poem and the chapter illustrate one possible approach to the text. I will elaborate on this approach later.

What other approaches are there? Obviously there is the *historical/critical* approach. It is this approach to which the

immediately preceding pages were devoted. Critical study is
essential for the preacher as a guard against the subjectivism
to which he or she can easily succumb. Word study, analysis,
and the rest, open one up to many possibilities in the hermeneutical task. But doing the historical/critical work is not itself
the function of preaching. At best it remains a tool.

It is helpful to know, for instance, that the Yahwist likely
took an old folk tale and made it into a vehicle for passing on
the story of faith. It is helpful because we discover thereby that
faith is not a static entity, but a living thing that needs renewal
in each generation. Yet this discovery, important as it is, does
not bring Jacob's story any closer to my experience than before.

Similarly, the following comment on Jacob's encounter on
the riverbank yields a helpful insight. "Commentators have
generally agreed on the significance of this experience for
Jacob as a dramatic turning point in his life."[22] Such a statement offers information about the work of scholars and, indi-
rectly, about Jacob's experience. It remains for the preacher to
link Jacob's experience with his or her own experience and
subsequently with the experience of those who will hear the
sermon.

The historical/critical approach deals with as much factual
data as can be ascertained by careful study. A limitation to this
approach is noted by James Hillman. Although Hillman is
referring to psychological, rather than biblical disciplines, his
comments bear on the hermeneutical task in preaching.

> The historical "facts" may be but fantasies attached to and
> sprouting from archetypical cores. Below the clouded and
> tangled pattern of events, and behind them, are experi-
> ences, psychological realities of passionate importance, a
> mythological substrate which gives the soul a feeling of
> destiny, an eschatological sense that *what happens matters.*
> And it matters to someone, to a person.[23]

Hillman's statement illustrates another approach to the text, an approach that emphasizes a *psychological* understanding. A book by John A. Sanford offers a recent example of this approach to Gen. 32:22–32. Its title and subtitle make plain the author's purpose: *The Man Who Wrestled With God: A study of individuation (personal growth toward wholeness) based on four Bible stories.*[24]

Rollo May, in his discussion of the daimonic, offers his own commentary on the story of Jacob at the Jabbok. As one might expect, this interpretation relies heavily on the language of May's own discipline. May identifies Jacob's adversary as a "daimon." He questions whether the daimon is a subjective projection on Jacob's part or an objective event such as imminent death. May answers that the daimon symbolizes both at the same time.

May gives special attention to the struggle of Jacob and what it means in psychological terms. Jacob was in conflict because of his imminent meeting with Esau. The daimon assaulted him at this precise time. Just so for all of us, it is inner conflict which brings the unconscious close to the surface. This opens up the channels to creativity. Jacob is thus the prototype of the creative person. May interprets Jacob's wound as symbolizing "that aspect of the creative experience which puts all of the man's self into it, calls forth an effort and level of consciousness which he did not know he could put forth, and leaves him crippled."[25]

A third approach to the text gives primary attention to the characteristics of *story*. Applying this approach to the account of Jacob, Stephen Crites suggests that rather than seek for the theological purpose of the storyteller, we would learn more by giving attention to the story itself. He argues that the changes in the legend did not occur at the hands of a "theological censor" determined to eliminate an alien theology, but by the "spontaneous artfulness" of an oral tradition over many generations.[26]

For Amos Wilder, the attempt to distill theological or psychological meanings from biblical stories was misguided. Wilder contended that metaphorical language could not be translated. He was especially critical of attempts to demythologize biblical stories. "Demythologizing," wrote Wilder, "fails to do justice to the meaning and truth of imagery. In waiving the wisdom of the myth for a supposed more fundamental meaning in terms of encounter, it seems to be motivated by a radical despair with respect to the possibilities of human knowing and even of Christian knowing."[27]

Another critic who favors giving primary attention to the story itself is James B. Wiggins. He advocates viewing stories as gifts. The mistake of theology has been to interpret the stories of a religion and then to treat the interpretation as if it were the primary reality. Stories that matter, argues Wiggins, outlive their own interpretations. To the objection that stories return us to the past and the limitations of the past, Wiggins replies that every encounter with a story is a present event. He agrees that some stories are created for didactic purposes, to persuade or convert. But, says Wiggins,

> a story of real importance is not an argument so much as it is a presentation and an invitation. It presents a realm of experience accessible through the imagination and invites participation in imaginative responses to reality, indeed to respond to reality as imaginative. A story invites one to tell one's own personal and collective stories in response. Stories evoke other stories.[28]

To regard the biblical stories as invitation is to move towards "personal, existential encounter with the biblical text," which I have described as "wrestling." To speak of story as inviting participation in imaginative responses is to open oneself to the dimension of the daimonic.

Two recent commentators on biblical stories exemplify in

their writings the kind of personal, existential encounter which I have attempted to describe. The first is Elie Wiesel, a survivor of a Nazi death camp. Wiesel is a storyteller who has written: "God made man because he loves stories."[29] In his stories Wiesel reveals his own inner strugle to make sense of traditional Jewish teachings about God. Dreams and demons haunt his fictional characters. The dark cloud of the Holocaust hangs over much of his writing. In his stories Wiesel grapples with the reality of good and evil both present and active in human experience.

It is not surprising, then, that his commentary on the story of Jacob on the riverbank should call forth from Wiesel reflections that reveal empathy with Jacob's struggle. Wiesel sifts through several rabbinical explanations for the identity of Jacob's attacker and then states his preference for the hypothesis that Jacob was attacked by his own guardian angel or the other half of Jacob's "split self," the side of him that had doubts about his mission, his future, his worthiness. Jacob took on this dark side of himself, and won. The primary meaning of the episode, then, is that "man's true victory is the one he achieves over himself." But, hold on, Wiesel says, an equally acceptable interpretation is that Jacob did battle, not with a self-image, but with God himself.[30] In the end, Jacob understood a "fundamental truth":

> God is in man, even in suffering, even in misfortune, even in evil. God is everywhere. In every being, not only in the victim. God does not wait for man at the end of the road, the termination of exile; He accompanies him there. More than that: He is the road, He is the exile. God holds both ends of the rope, He is present in every extremity, He is every limit. He is part of Jacob and He is part of Esau.[31]

In that paragraph Wiesel reveals what his own struggle with the story has produced. The language, the imagery, are not simply the product of biblical scholarship or psychological insight but the result of Wiesel's imaginative response to the story. As he states in his preface, it is his aim as a storyteller to reacquaint himself with the stories of his people and then to "insert them into the present." For, says Wiesel, "all the legends, all the stories . . . involve us." The legends the storyteller transmits are "the very ones we are living today."[32]

The second commentator on our text to whom I turn is Arthur I. Waskow. Waskow is also Jewish, although until his forties he was a secular intellectual and left-wing activist with little knowledge of biblical Hebrew or the Torah. A subsequent study of them brought about a significant change in his life. In his book *Godwrestling* he documents the upheavals in his thinking that grew out of his encounter with his faith tradition.

In dealing with the story of Jacob's conflict with Esau, Waskow is reminded of his own lifelong relationship with his brother. But he moves from reflection on that very human encounter to the dimension of transcendence. For what Jacob encountered in his nighttime wrestling match was the question: Why must it be this way? Why do I need to cheat my brother in order to make my way in the world? Why must my will conflict with another's will? And only when Jacob struggled against this reality of Things-As-They-Must-Be, only when "he dared to wrestle with God, knowing that it was indeed God and not mere human wants and wishes he was wrestling with," only then could the war of brothers be turned into love.[33]

What the story reveals, Waskow asserts, is that there are not two utterly separate and diametrically opposed forces in the world, but One. And only by wrestling can we learn that truth.

> To wrestle with God is to make in human action and on the human level the same unification of the opposites that God unifies. It is a way of bringing to visibility that paradoxical Image of God which is stamped deep within us. For

to wrestle with God is also to wrestle with human beings —
ourselves and others. It is to face polarities and unify them.[34]

It seems more than coincidental that Wiesel and Waskow
can write so powerfully about Jacob's struggle. Their own
life-wrestlings enabled them to move into the story and to
bring from it insights that, for me at least, are profoundly
moving.

My own wrestling with the text resulted in the drama/
sermon which follows. There are three characters in the drama.
The first is the Storyteller who provides an introduction and
then literally takes the role of storyteller. By telling rather
than reading the text, the Storyteller gives an immediacy to
Jacob's story.[35] Rather than confine the drama/sermon to the
struggle on the riverbank, I drew on the total Jacob narrative,
in order to set the final struggle in context and in order to
reveal Jacob's humanity — his hopes, fears, weaknesses, acts of
courage, and sense of being wronged. The remaining two characters, Jacob and the Observer, personify the struggle that is an
essential part of the story and reaches its climax in the last
scene.

The character of the Observer can be seen as our logical,
rational side. He uses his intellectualizing as a defense against
Godwrestling. In our encounter with a text, especially as we
approach it critically, we are naturally pulled towards a rational interpretation. As I have previously indicated, this is a
necessary step. The danger is that we remain there. The Observer makes a number of important observations about Jacob,
enough to convince us that he possesses insight into the human
psyche. He notes Jacob's mixed motives. He interprets Jacob's
behavior, or to use the vernacular, *psyches him out*. But the
Observer will not admit to the possibility of transcendence.

It is this refusal that the Jacob character renounces. Jacob
bears in silence the often caustic remarks of the Observer until

the end of the play. He remains "frozen," unable to respond. This dramatic device suggests that Jacob passively accepts the criticism of the parent-figure, internalizes it, perhaps attributes it to God as Parent. But in the riverbank encounter, Jacob discovers resources within himself he was not aware of. Having confronted God "face-to-face," Jacob knows with certainty that the haranguing voice of the Observer is not God's voice. Neither will he tolerate any longer the "sterile rage" of the Observer which cloaks itself in an intellectualized I'm-just-doing-this-for-your-own-good attitude. Jacob, now as twentieth century character, turns his anger against the mechanistic, demythologized secularism that has left us without moorings.

The play ends in affirmation. Jacob tells us that his struggle was with God, that it was God who stalked him and not vice versa, and that he, Jacob, responded. He could have chosen not to respond, not to wrestle. It was a genuine risk, for Jacob as well as for God. By choosing to wrestle with God, Jacob discovers his true self, or better, has his true self "thrust upon him."

All this is not to say there is no ambiguity at the end. The title of the play is purposely ambiguous. *Who* came to Peniel? Jacob? God? Myself? Yes. And whoever it was came to Peniel, their leaving of Peniel left them changed.

Even God? If the crucifixion of Jesus tells us anything, it says that God makes himself vulnerable to us, that our striving with God leaves God marked, beaten, wounded. The Genesis story of God's wrestling match with Jacob, in this sense, prefigures the cross.

There remains one mystery. It is the same one met in the exegesis of the text. Who is the one who encounters Jacob? Who is the One who risks all at the Jabbok, on Calvary, in the here and now? Any answer given should not attempt to expunge the mystery. Arthur Waskow, in the opening chapter of *Godwrestling*, expresses what any preacher might also offer by way of answer.

Who is this God we wrestle? One whose face is as hard to recognize as my brother's. Or as my own, the face I have never seen. One who wishes to be faced, who needs to be wrestled. One whose Self is not complete, not self-sufficient.

I have only begun to learn that Face, begun to learn it only from the struggles of my life. I welcome wrestling partners to this book. Together we may be able to see the outlines of God's Face. And of each other's.[36]

He Came to Peniel
A Drama/Sermon

STORYTELLER: Crafty, romantic, pious, brazen, devious—these are but a few words which describe the character of the Hebrew patriarch Jacob. The book of Genesis tells his story, and it is one of the most fascinating stories told anywhere. Today we will meet Jacob, this twin who treacherously stole his brother's birthright, this man of ambition who outwitted his greedy uncle Laban, this descendant of Abraham who, the legend tells us, lost or maybe won a wrestling match with God himself. We will hear Jacob's story as the Bible tells it, we will listen to the thoughts of Jacob, and we will reflect on his story as we hear one who is an Observer tell of it. Remember, as you listen, this is the story of Jacob, a father of the faith, a man through whom God's promises came to eventual fulfillment. This is the story of Jacob, whose name was changed. This is the story of Jacob, who one dark night became Israel, for he strove with God and men . . . and prevailed.

I

[STORYTELLER *begins reading from the Bible he/she is holding. After several sentences,* STORYTELLER *closes Bible and continues telling the story from memory.*]

(Gen. 28:10–15)

STORYTELLER: Jacob left Beersheba, and went toward Haran.

[JACOB *enters and lies down*]

And he came to a certain place and stayed there that

night, because the sun had set. Taking one of the stones
of the place, he put it under his head and lay down in that
place to sleep. And he dreamed that there was a ladder set
up on the earth, and the top of it reached to heaven; and
behold, the angels of God were ascending and descending
on it! And behold, the Lord stood above it and said, "I am
the Lord, the God of Abraham your father and the God
of Isaac; the land on which you lie I will give to you and
to your descendants; and your descendants shall be like
the dust of the earth, and you shall spread abroad to the
west and to the east and to the north and to the south; and
by you and your descendants shall all the families of the
earth bless themselves. Behold, I am with you and will
keep you wherever you go, and will bring you back to this
land.

JACOB: [*In dreamlike state*]
What is this I see?
A ladder, reaching up and up . . .
heavenward.
Or maybe—down and down . . .
earthward.
A riddle then, this dream.
Dream . . . or vision. . . .
It *is* a dream, of course.
I know it is a dream because . . .
. . . because . . .
because I am asleep . . .
or was at least. And because
a thing like this I have not seen before.
A ladder going nowhere
going somewhere
going anywhere!
Is that the riddle?
Yes and no. For there is another too.
Does the ladder reach from heaven down,

or upwards, from the earth?
Is it there for me to climb,
or will some one climb down?
Shall I act, or shall I wait and see?
Shall I go, or shall I stay right here?
Shall I act, or shall I wait and see?
Shall I go, or shall I stay right here?
It spins, this ladder, floats before my eyes.
Shall I act or . . .?
A mystery, riddle, dream . . .
shall I go, or shall I . . .
a mystery, dream, a riddle . . .
shall I . . . or should I . . . or . . .
Stop! *I HATE RIDDLES!*

(Gen. 28:16a,17a)

STORYTELLER: Then Jacob awoke from his sleep . . . and he
was afraid . . .

JACOB: Where am I?
What is this place?
A place possessed, a dream-haunted spot.
Yes.
I fear it, fear this darkness.
It is lonely here.
A bad place for a dream.
A dream—what was it?
Bright beings, angels—on a ladder!
A ladder going up and down, down and up.
And angels on it, going up and down.
A voice then.
I swear it was the voice of El himself!
Surely he is *in* this place
and I knew it not.
This is none other than the house of God,
and this the gate of heaven.

[*Kneels with forehead touching floor, remains "frozen"
throughout* OBSERVER'S *speech.*]

OBSERVER: But it was only a dream, Jacob. Don't take it so
seriously, man! Have you never had a dream before? They
say some people never dream, or at least never remember
a dream. Maybe you're one of those. Or at least you were
till this ladder thing came along. Your kind has no time
for dreams.

A man of the world, that's you. Always a sharp eye for
the main chance. Cheated your brother Esau of his inheri-
tance. Oh yes, it was your mother's idea. But yours was
the pocket fattened, yours the birthright gained. And so
you ran away—your brother swore to kill you. No wonder you have fearful dreams, Jacob. A guilty conscience
maybe?

Jacob, are you running away? Or are you running towards something? Should you act or should you wait and
see? Should you go or should you stay right here?

That is always the question in life, is it not, Jacob my
friend? It's what we all struggle to answer, time and time
again. You're not the first to face it, nor the last. Don't
overdramatize things! It's just life you saw in your dream,
that's all.

Angels? The voice of God? There, you see, that's what
I mean by overdramatizing! I suppose there's no harm in
it though. A religious high every now and then—all right.
But don't overdo it.

Beth-el. The House of God. That's the name you gave
this place of dreams. Well, okay, Jacob, if that makes you
happy. But morning comes round every morning. You
can't stay on the mountain; none of us can—more's the
pity. That's just the way it is. Soon Beth-el will be far
behind, Jacob. What then? We will see, Jacob. We will
see.

II
(Gen. 29:16–20)

STORYTELLER: Now Laban had two daughters; the name of the
older was Leah, and the name of the younger was Rachel.
Leah's eyes were weak, but Rachel was beautiful and
lovely. Jacob loved Rachel; and he said, "I will serve you
seven years for your younger daughter Rachel." Laban
said, "It is better that I give her to you than that I should
give her to any other man; stay with me." So Jacob served
seven years for Rachel, and they seemed to him but a few
days because of the love he had for her.

JACOB: You cannot hear me, Rachel, my dearest.
You sleep tonight inside your father's house.
But never again, after this night,
I vow by this bounding heart inside my chest,
never will we sleep apart again.
Tomorrow you shall be my wife!
And tomorrow and tomorrow after that,
for a thousand tomorrows,
we will be together.
You were but a child when first I saw you,
Rachel. There at the well with your father's flock.
I kissed you then — remember?
A kinsman's kiss, that's all.
But even then it held the promise
of something that would be.
A child you were — in face and form.
But even then I saw in you
the woman that would be.
Yet never did I dream that you would
grow into the goddess you are now!
Never has there been a fairer bride
than you, my dearest wife-to-be.
They called me fool back then,
when they heard about my pledge.

"Work seven years for that scrawny kid!"
was the gist.
I heard them laughing in their tents.
They are not laughing anymore, my love.
Rachel, sleep well upon your bed.
Dream and see the joy that will be ours.
I may not sleep at all tonight, myself.
My heart is much too full.

[*Freezes into position for duration of* OBSERVER'ᴗ *speech.*]

OBSERVER: Dreams again, Jacob? For one who never dreams,
you seem to talk about them overmuch. I think this time
we can excuse you though. Lovers have the right to dream.
You've earned it too. Entranced by love you indentured
yourself seven years to your uncle Laban. You say the
years flew by—maybe they did. But in that span of time
you've learned a trick or two. Learned your uncle is a
grasping, greedy cheat. Learned too how to turn his greed
to your own purpose. Yet all the time he had you where
he wanted you. Rachel was his daughter, and what you
wouldn't do for her! Remember that, and beware. Your
uncle has one more trick up his sleeve.

Not only uncles but fate itself deceives us, friend Jacob.
Your visions of wedded bliss seem so real. And they will
be, for a time. But unlike you, I can see what's coming
down the road. Not just one wife, but two. With children,
servants, cattle, you are destined to become a man of
property, a family man, with more duty and care than you
can dream of now. It will weary you, cost you a different
kind of sleepless night than this.

But don't worry about that now, Jacob. Keep your vigil
of love.

III

(Gen. 30:25–26, 29–30; 31:1–3)

STORYTELLER: When Rachel had borne Joseph, Jacob said to
Laban, "Send me away that I may go to my own home and

country. Give me my wives and my children for whom I have served you, and let me go; for you know the service which I have given you."

Jacob said to him, "You yourself know how I have served you, and how your cattle have fared with me. For you had little before I came, and it has increased abundantly; and the Lord has blessed you wherever I turned. But now when shall I provide for my own household also?"

Now Jacob heard that the sons of Laban were saying, "Jacob has taken all that was our father's; and from what was our father's he has gained all his wealth." And Jacob saw that Laban did not regard him with favor as before. Then the Lord said to Jacob, "Return to the land of your fathers and to your kindred, and I will be with you."

JACOB: Leah, Rachel—come here—now!
Now listen . . . we're going to leave,
get out of here for good.
I will be treated like a thief no longer.
Laban's sons, your brothers, are starting up again.
"Jacob's wealth was stolen from our father,"
this they say. "Jacob is a cheat, a thief."
I tell you I will stand for it no more.
Calm down, you say? Calm down?
You know the truth in this as well as I!
From the day I showed my face to him
he's taken every chance to play me false.
Seven years I worked for Rachel's hand.
Seven years!
And then he gives me Leah in her place!
Leah, stop it now.
You know I don't blame you.
Besides, it happened long ago.
You gave me sons—a progeny to make proud any man.
I hold against you no complaint at all.

Laban is the one who is to blame.
A conniving cheat!
You remember once before
I told him I would leave.
I asked him for an honest wage.
"Yes, my son-in-law," he said,
"take all the spotted sheep among the flock;
this will be my wage and farewell gift."
And then behind my back, he drove
the spotted sheep away.
If I have prospered here,
it is no thanks to him!
I've worked for what is mine.
The lies your brothers tell are based on greed,
that and jealousy, my wives.
I'm weary onto death of Laban and his sons.
Go . . . get your things together.
Tell the children they must help you too.

And so the die is cast. We're going.
I could not tell them of the voice I heard.
"Return onto your father's land," it said.
(I think that's what it said.)
The self-same voice that came to me that night
of dreams. Beth El! The house of God!
I have not given thought to that in years.
The voice that night pledged sons,
children many as the dust of earth.
It promised too that wealth would heap high.
Was it God then? I cannot know.
But I know this:
when Laban said, "The spotted sheep are yours,"
then all the ewes bore lambs of spotted mark.
And when he said, "The striped shall be your pay,"
then it was that all the flock bore striped.

It's true. All this *has* come to pass!
The promise is fulfilled.
My sojourn in this hostile land is done.
Besides, I fear the angry buzz of Laban's sons.
They'd kill me if they weren't such craven curs.

Leah, tell Reub and Simeon to give you help.
And Rachel, where is Joseph?
I want him here beside me while I pack.
[*Exit* JACOB]

OBSERVER: Jacob is an interesting fellow, really. And as consistent as they come. Once again he thinks he is going somewhere, when in reality he's running away, just as before. You think I'm too hard on him? Ah hah, he's charmed you with that "little boy lost" routine. It's the same thing that made his mother dote on him. Even poor Leah mothers him, and all the while she knows he despises her. Well, I grant you Jacob does have charm. How else can we account for the Almighty's indulgence of him, even favoritism? Now me, I don't charm easily. I've seen Jacob's kind before. So have you. Always telling you how hard he's got it, how the cost of living will drive him to the wall. And as you listen, you keep thinking about that beautiful home he's living in, the big car he drives, the vacation he took last winter in Rio. Jacob protests a little too much for my taste. Still, everyone to his or her own taste. Live and let live. Okay, okay.

But admit this much, anyway. Jacob is hardly a religious man—*until* he runs into trouble. As long as things are going well, he's cool, a self-made man. Then problems come and—zip—he's back talking about God again. You watch. If things get hot, we'll see him on his knees, asking God the Lord to bail him out.

Hard to believe this man is a father of the faith. God knows *I* wouldn't have picked him.

IV
(Gen. 32:6–9, 11, 22–31)

STORYTELLER: And the messengers returned to Jacob, saying, "We came to your brother Esau, and he is coming to meet you, and four hundred men with him." Then Jacob was greatly afraid and distressed; and he divided his people that were with him, and the flocks and herds and camels, into two companies, thinking, "If Esau comes to the one company and destroys it, then the company which is left will escape." And Jacob said, "O God of my father Abraham and God of my father Isaac. . . . Deliver me, I pray thee, from the hand of my brother, from the hand of Esau, for I fear him, lest he come and slay us all, the mothers with the children." The same night he arose and took his two wives, his two maids, and his eleven children, and crossed the ford of the Jabbok. He took them and set them across the stream, and likewise everything that he had. And Jacob was left alone; and a man wrestled with him until the breaking of the day. When the man saw that he did not prevail against Jacob, he touched the hollow of his thigh; and Jacob's thigh was put out of joint as he wrestled with him. Then he said, "Let me go, for the day is breaking." But Jacob said, "I will not let you go, unless you bless me." And he said to him, "What is your name?" And he said, "Jacob." Then he said, "Your name shall no more be called Jacob, but Israel, for you have striven with God and with men, and have prevailed." Then Jacob asked him, "Tell me, I pray, your name." But he said, "Why is it that you ask my name?" And there he blessed him. So Jacob called the name of the place Peniel, saying, "For I have seen God face to face, and yet my life is preserved." The sun rose upon him as he passed Peniel, limping because of his thigh.

OBSERVER: Now let me tell you what all that means. Jacob was frightened, right? But wait, not just frightened—he was

terrified. He hears Esau is coming to meet him with four
hundred men. The guilt of his long-ago treachery towards
[JACOB *enters, unseen by* OBSERVER]
his brother comes rushing back. It overwhelms him. In
desperation to do something—anything—he does two
things. First, he divides his retinue into two companies.
(What good will that do?) And second, he prays. (Told you
so!) These desperate measures do no good. As daylight
fades, his terror rises to the frantic point. Ashamed to have
others see him fall apart, he sends his servants, children,
Leah, and even Rachel, across the stream.

You have heard of men "beside themselves" with fear?
There in the darkness, Jacob grappled with his other self.
The dark, fearful self that lodges in each one of us. It was
a fight for sanity, a life and death struggle. When it was
done, at last, Jacob was a changed man. That's the
significance of the new name—Israel.

Was the whole thing just another dream? Well, maybe
and maybe not. The symbolism of the whole thing
is really very interesting. A Freudian analysis reveals
that . . .

JACOB: [*To* OBSERVER]
No. We'll have no more of this.
You would strip the story bare,
pick it to the bones.
Then with satiated belch
you mourn the dearth of passion in the world.
Enraged because you have
no story of your own to tell,
you turn your sterile rage upon
the men who do.
Your world is swept clean
of heroes, villains, God.
You are a man without a story,
without a truth.

I pity you.
[*To audience*]
It's true I was afraid.
No shame in that.
The night was black as pitch.
Moon bare.
Stars burned coldly overhead.
I sensed a presence there
before I felt its touch.
You talk of fear!
My hair stood straight up from my head.
Without a word, he grasped my throat.
And I can tell you
no apparition ever gripped like that!
We strove, till sinews cracked,
without a word between us.
Long.
Exhausted.
The sky grayed then.
He asked to be released.
I begged a blessing first.
I asked him for his name.
He said just this:
"Why is it that you ask my name?"

Who was it then, you say?
The legends tell us
El will bide his time.
Then he comes.
Some receive him
arms outstretched in greeting.
Some — the cowardly,
the ignorant, the proud —
must needs be pounced upon

and pummeled to the ground.
Such a one was I.

I named the place Peni El.
It means "the Face of God."

That's all there is to tell
for now, at least.
Except—I am no longer Jacob.
My name is Isra El,
"He who strives with God."
I did not choose the name myself.
You might say
I had it thrust upon me.
[*Exit—with noticeable limp*]

A Concluding Word:
The Preacher as Jacob

To identify the preacher with Jacob is to indulge in metaphor. Like all metaphors, this one has its limitations. Nevertheless, there is a sense in which all of us whose identities are shaped by the preaching vocation have had that vocation "thrust upon us." Preaching is not something we choose to do. Who, indeed, would choose, would dare, to stand in front of the people and presume to utter the word of the Lord? Jeremiah speaks for every preacher.

> If I say, "I will not mention him
>   or speak any more in his name,"
> There is in my heart as it were a burning fire
>   shut up in my bones,
>   and I am weary with holding it in,
>   and I cannot (Jer. 20:9).

And so we speak of being *called* to preach, of having *hands laid upon* us. These too are metaphors, and they point to *encounter* as paradigmatic for the preacher. We who preach must therefore not suppose we will be spared the struggle. If we choose, of course, we can avoid the loneliness of the dark riverbank. We can instead stroll down pleasant garden paths and proffer equally pleasant homilies. We can plod along tried and true trails of banal moralisms. We can even walk the burning-social-issues picket line of prophetic exhortation. If we choose such routes, we may speak words of comfort and encouragement and challenge.

But only if we risk the daimonic encounter will our preaching be invested with the power that comes from beyond ourselves, that bears the mark of transcendence. Wrestling with the daimonic is not a luxury we indulge in on special occasions. It is the indispensable element in proclaiming the word of God. Without such encounter, what we say is not preaching at all. It is something less. And something less simply will not do. It will not and cannot save.

NOTES

Introduction

[1]Rollo May, *Love and Will* (New York: W. W. Norton, 1969), p. 123.
[2]Rainer Maria Rilke, Letter 74, *Briefe aus den Jahren 1907 bis 1914.*
[3]May, p. 134.
[4]Madeleine L'Engle, *The Irrational Season* (New York: Seabury Press, 1977),
  p. 76.
[5]May, p. 171.

Chapter I

[1]*The Interpreter's Dictionary of the Bible,* s.v. "Demon," by T. H. Gaster
  (New York: Abingdon Press, 1962), Vol. 1, p. 817.
[2]Ibid.
[3]Ibid.
[4]Henry Ansgar Kelly, *Towards the Death of Satan* (London: Geoffrey Chap-
  man, 1968), p. 3.
[5]*A Dictionary of Comparative Religion,* s.v. "Demons," by S. G. F. Brandon
  (London: Weidenfeld and Nicholson, 1970), p. 231.
[6]*Interpreter's Dictionary,* Vol. 1, p. 819.
[7]Ibid., Vol. 1, p. 818.
[8]Kelly, p. 6.
[9]*Interpreter's Dictionary,* Vol. 1, p. 822.
[10]*Encyclopedia of Biblical Theology,* s.v. "Demon," by Johann Michl (London: Sheed and Ward, 1970), Vol. 1, p. 193.
[11]Kelly, p. 11.
[12]See 1 Tim. 4:1 and 1 John 4:6.

¹³*Dictionary of the Bible*, s.v. "Demon," by John L.McKenzie (Milwaukee: The Bruce Publishing Company, 1965), p. 193.

¹⁴E. R. Dodds, *The Greeks and the Irrational* (Berkeley: University of California Press, 1968), p. 11.

¹⁵Ibid., p. 41.

¹⁶Ibid., p. 185.

¹⁷Rollo May, *Love and Will*, pp. 137–138.

Chapter II

¹Rollo May, *Love and Will*, p. 123.

²Ibid., p. 125.

³William Butler Yeats, "Fergus and the Druid," *The Variorum Edition of the Poems of W. B. Yeats*, eds., Peter Allt and Russell K. Alspach (New York: Macmillan, 1957), p. 104.

⁴May, p. 123.

⁵Sigmund Freud, *Collected Papers*, 5 vols., trans. Alix and James Strachey (New York: Basic Books, 1959), 3:132.

⁶Douglas N. Morgan, *Love: Plato, the Bible and Freud* (Englewood Cliffs: Prentice-Hall, Inc., 1964), p. 158.

⁷C. G. Jung, *The Collected Works of C. G. Jung*, trans. R. F. C. Hull, vol. 11: *Psychology and Religion: West and East*, Bollingen Series, no. 20 (New York: Pantheon Books, Inc., 1958), p. 334.

⁸Ann and Barry Ulanov, *Religion and the Unconscious* (Philadelphia: The Westminster Press, 1975), p. 67.

⁹C. G. Jung, *The Collected Works of C. G. Jung*, trans. R. F. C. Hull, vol. 9, part 2: *Aion*, Bollingen Series, no. 20 (New York: Pantheon Books, Inc., 1959), p. 8.

¹⁰Jung, *Psychology and Religion*, p. 76.

¹¹Jung, *Aion*, p. 9.

¹²Jung, *Psychology and Religion*, p. 83.

¹³Ibid., p. 78.

¹⁴Ibid., p. 339.

¹⁵Ibid., p. 357.

¹⁶Ann Ulanov, "The Psychological Reality of the Demonic," in *Disguises of the Demonic*, ed. Alan M. Olson (New York: Association Press, 1975), p. 135.

¹⁷C. G. Jung, *The Collected Works of C. G. Jung*, trans. R. F. C. Hull, vol. 10: *Civilization in Transition*, Bollingen Series, no. 20 (New York: Pantheon Books, Inc., 1964), p. 447. Jung's description of the conscience is reminiscent of W. B. Yeats' description of the daimonic noted by Rollo May. Writes May: "We could never apply to conscience Yeats' definition of the

daimonic—that 'other Will,' 'that dazzling, unforeseen wing-footed wanderer ...' " Cited in May, p. 124.

[18]Ulanov, "Psychological Reality," p. 143. Similarly, John A. Sanford states: "Possession by the unconscious takes place in direct relationship to our psychological ignorance of ourselves. We are most taken over, therefore, by what we do not recognize and understand. . . . For this reason all manner of evil is perpetrated in the name of good, and fantastic forms of deviltry have been done in the name of God. In our own time, possession by the shadow is a great danger. To live out our darkest urges compulsively and unconsciously is to become possessed by evil. . . . The violence of our wars, the increase of crime, greed, the lust for power that has taken over our highest political offices, and the destruction of our environment all attest to possession by the shadow." John A. Sanford, *Healing and Wholeness* (New York: Paulist Press, 1977), p. 101.

[19]Ulanov, "Psychological Reality," p. 143.

[20]Ibid., p. 148.

[21]May, p. 159.

[22]Ibid., p. 163.

[23]Ibid., p. 176.

[24]Paul Tillich, "The Philosophy of Religion," in *What Is Religion?* ed. James Luther Adams (New York: Harper & Row, Publishers, 1969), p. 85.

[25]Paul Tillich, *The Interpretation of History* (New York: Charles Scribner's Sons, 1936), p. 81.

[26]Ibid., p. 90.

[27]Ibid., p. 88.

[28]Ibid., p. 93.

[29]Ibid., p. 96.

[30]Ibid., p. 26.

[31]Paul Tillich, *The Courage to Be* (New Haven: Yale University Press, 1952), p. 122.

[32]Paul Tillich, *Systematic Theology*, 3 vols. in 1 (Chicago: University of Chicago Press, 1967), 3:51.

[33]Ibid., 3:102.

[34]Ibid., 3:105.

[35]Ibid., 3:110.

[36]Francis J. Molson, "The Earthsea Trilogy," in *Ursula K. LeGuin, Voyager to Inner Lands and to Outer Space*, ed. Joe De Bolt (Port Washington, N.Y.: Kennikat Press, 1979), p. 129.

[37]Paul Walker, "Ursula K. LeGuin: An Interview," *Luna Monthly*, March 1976, p. 2.

[38]Ursula K. LeGuin, *Dreams Must Explain Themselves* (New York: Algol Press, 1975), p. 11.

[39]Ibid., p. 12.

[40]Ursula K. LeGuin, *A Wizard of Earthsea* (New York: Bantam Books, Inc., 1975), p. 2.

[41]Ibid., p. 23.

[42]Ibid., p. 179.

[43]Rollin A. Lasseter, "Four Letters about LeGuin," in *Voyager to Inner Lands*, p. 96.

[44]Ursula K. LeGuin, *The Language of the Night*, ed. Susan Wood (New York: G. P. Putnam's Sons, 1979), p. 64.

[45]Ibid., p. 65.

[46]Ibid., p. 70.

[47]Ibid., p. 44.

[48]LeGuin, *Wizard*, p. 128.

[49]Ibid., p. 129.

[50]LeGuin, *The Language of the Night*, p. 124.

Chapter III

[1]Richard A. Jensen, *Telling the Story: Variety and Imagination in Preaching* (Minneapolis: Augsburg Publishing House, 1980), p. 67.

[2]Clyde Fant, *Preaching for Today* (New York: Harper & Row, 1975), p. 113.

[3]"The classic 'three-point sermon' . . . all too frequently turns out to be three independent statements developed at some length with some relationship to a central theme. . . . The legacy of the nineteenth-century pulpit, with its characteristic announcement of the theme at the beginning of the sermon along with the major divisions or heads, has laid a dreary hand on much of the preaching still done today." Edmund A. Steimle, "The Fabric of the Sermon," in *Preaching the Story*, Edmund A. Steimle, Morris J. Niedenthal, and Charles L. Rice (Philadelphia: Fortress Press, 1980), p. 171.

"I suspect that for many preachers putting a sermon together is a weekly matter of *rearranging* a biblical text so that it fits into a prefabricated, three-point mold. To the extent that that is true for us our sermon preparation owes far more of its shape to Greek rhetoric and Gutenberg linearity than it does to the particular literary form of the biblical text that is before us." Jensen, p. 34.

[4]Fred B. Craddock, *As One Without Authority* (Enid, Oklahoma: Phillips University Press, 1974), p. 56.

[5]Ibid., p. 62.

[6]Ibid., p. 64.

Eugene L. Lowry, *The Homiletical Plot: The Sermon as Narrative Art Form* (Atlanta: John Knox Press, 1980), p. 12.

[8]Ibid., p. 15.

[9]Charles L. Rice, *Interpretation and Imagination: The Preacher and Contemporary Literature,* The Preacher's Paperback Library (Philadelphia: Fortress Press, 1970), p. 65.

[10]Morris J. Niedenthal and Charles L. Rice, "Preaching as Shared Story," in *Preaching the Story,* p. 13.

[11]Lowry, p. 15.

[12]Hans van der Geest, *Presence in the Pulpit: The Impact of Personality in Preaching,* trans. Douglas W. Scott (Atlanta: John Knox Press, 1981), p. 147.

[13]Frederick Buechner, in an interview with the author, 10 November 1982.

[14]Frederick Buechner, *Telling the Truth: The Gospel as Tragedy, Comedy, and Fairy Tale* (New York: Harper & Row, 1977), p. 24.

[15]See the introductory chapter, "My Story, Your Story, His Story," in my book, *Yeast, Salt, and Secret Agents* (Elgin: The Brethren Press, 1979), pp. 13–16.

[16]A partial listing of such works includes:

Frederick Buechner, *Telling the Truth: The Gospel as Tragedy, Comedy, and Fairy Tale* (New York: Harper & Row, 1977).

Fred B. Craddock, *As One Without Authority* (Enid, Oklahoma: Phillips University Press, 1974).

———, *Overhearing the Gospel* (Nashville: Abingdon, 1978).

John Dominic Crossan, *The Dark Interval: Towards a Theology of Story* (Niles, Illinois: Argus Communications, 1975).

Robert W. Funk, *Jesus as Precursor* (Philadelphia: Fortress Press, 1975).

Warren F. Groff, *Story Time: God's Story and Ours* (Elgin: The Brethren Press, 1974).

Richard A. Jensen, *Telling the Story: Variety and Imagination in Preaching* (Minneapolis: Augsburg Publishing House, 1980).

Eugene L. Lowry, *The Homiletical Plot: The Sermon as Narrative Art Form* (Atlanta: John Knox Press, 1980).

Edmund A. Steimle, Morris J. Niedenthal, and Charles L. Rice, *Preaching the Story* (Philadelphia: Fortress Press, 1980).

James B. Wiggins, ed., *Religion As Story* (New York: Harper & Row, 1975).

[17]Ronald J. Allen and Thomas J. Herin, "Moving from The Story to Our Story," in *Preaching the Story,* p. 161.

[18]Charles L. Rice, *Interpretation and Imagination,* p. 86.

[19]Frederick Buechner, *Telling the Truth,* p. 98.

[20]See, for instance:

Howard E. Gruber et al., eds., *Contemporary Approaches to Creative Thinking* (New York: Atherton Press, 1962).

Arthur Koestler, *The Act of Creation* (New York: Macmillan, 1964).

Rollo May, *The Courage to Create* (New York: W. W. Norton, 1975).

Henrik M. Ruitenbeek, ed., *The Creative Imagination: Psychoanalysis and the Genius of Inspiration* (Chicago: Quadrangle Books, 1965).

Vincent Tomas, ed., *Creativity in the Arts* (Englewood Cliffs: Prentice-Hall, Inc., 1964).

[21]Dorothy Sayers, *The Mind of the Maker* (New York: Harcourt, Brace, 1941), p. xiv.

[22]Ibid., pp. 38–41.

[23]Stephen Spender, "The Making of a Poem," in *Creativity in the Arts*, ed. Vincent Tomas, Prentice-Hall Contemporary Perspectives in Philosophy Series, Joel Feinberg and Wesley C. Salmon, eds. (Englewood Cliffs: Prentice-Hall, Inc., 1964), p. 41.

[24]Elizabeth Achtemeier, *Creative Preaching: Finding the Words*, ed. William D. Thompson, Abingdon Preacher's Library (Nashville: Abingdon, 1980), pp. 22–43.

[25]Ibid., p. 117.

[26]Robert D. Young, *Religious Imagination: God's Gift to Prophets and Preachers* (Philadelphia: Westminster Press, 1979), p. 25.

[27]Lowry, p. 65.

[28]Ibid., p. 85.

[29]Rollo May, *The Courage to Create* (New York: W. W. Norton, 1975), p. 76.

[30]Arthur Gordon, "Six Hours with Rudyard Kipling," in *How to Live with Life* (Pleasantville, New York: the Reader's Digest Association, 1965).

[31]Rollo May, "Creativity and Encounter," in *The Creative Imagination: Psychoanalysis and the Genius of Inspiration*, ed. Henrik M. Ruitenbeek (Chicago: Quadrangle Books, 1965), p. 289.

[32]Ibid., p. 284.

[33]Ibid., p. 290.

Chapter IV

[1]Henri J. M. Nouwen, *Creative Ministry* (Garden City: Doubleday & Company, Inc., 1971), p. 34.

[2]Ibid., p. 35.

[3]Charles L. Rice, "The Preacher's Story," in *Preaching the Story*, Edmund A. Steimle, Morris J. Niedenthal, and Charles L. Rice (Philadelphia: Fortress Press, 1980), p. 26.

[4]Kenneth L. Gibble, "Should Dunkers Be Different?" *Messenger*, November, 1982, p. 18.

[5]Of great practical help in understanding dreams is Ann Faraday, *The Dream Game* (New York: Harper & Row, 1976). Two books which offer a theological understanding of dreams are Morton T. Kelsey, *Dreams: The Dark Speech of the Spirit* (Garden City: Doubleday & Company, Inc., 1968) and John A. Sanford, *Dreams: God's Forgotten Language* (New York: J. B. Lippincott Company, 1968).

[6]C. G. Jung, *The Collected Works of C. G. Jung*, trans. R. F. C. Hull, vol. 10: *Civilization in Transition*, Bollingen Series, no. 20 (New York: Pantheon Books, Inc., 1964), p. 151.

[7]Michael Williams, "Storytelling and the Family: a Conversation with Gerry Armstrong and Rebecca Shepherd," *Explore* 5 (Fall 1979):58.

[8]Frederick Buechner, in an interview with the author, 10 November 1982.

[9]Madeleine L'Engle, *Walking on Water: Reflections on Faith and Art* (Wheaton: Harold Shaw Publishers, 1980), p. 13.

[10]Kenneth L. Gibble, "Loving the Shadow," sermon delivered at the Ridgeway Community Church of the Brethren, Harrisburg, Pennsylvania, 30 November 1980.

[11]Kenneth L. Gibble, "If I Should Die . . . Clues to the New Creation," sermon delivered at the 194th Church of the Brethren Annual Conference, Pittsburgh, Pennsylvania, 25 June 1980.

[12]Ibid.

[13]Richard A. Jensen, *Telling the Story: Variety and Imagination in Preaching* (Minneapolis: Augsburg Publishing House, 1980), p. 131.

[14]Kenneth L. Gibble, meditation delivered at the memorial service for Sanford F. Zug, Ridgeway Community Church of the Brethren, Harrisburg, Pennsylvania, 9 March 1978.

[15]Kenneth L. Gibble, "What a Waste," sermon delivered at the Ridgeway Community Church of the Brethren, Harrisburg, Pennsylvania, 4 January 1981.

[16]Kenneth L. Gibble, "Sparring at the Well," sermon delivered at the Ridgeway Community Church of the Brethren, Harrisburg, Pennsylvania, 14 March 1981.

[17]Kenneth L. Gibble, *Yeast, Salt, and Secret Agents* (Elgin: The Brethren Press, 1979), p. 81.

[18]Kenneth L. Gibble, "A God Who Terrifies," sermon delivered at the Ridgeway Community Church of the Brethren, Harrisburg, Pennsylvania, 7 November 1982.

[19]Jensen, pp. 152–53.

[20]Hans van der Geest, *Presence in the Pulpit: The Impact of Personality in Preaching*, trans. Douglas W. Scott (Atlanta: John Knox Press, 1981), p. 80.

[21]Sallie TeSelle, *Speaking in Parables* (Philadelphia: Fortress Press, 1975), p. 150.

[22]Kenneth L. Gibble, "Christ the Light," sermon delivered at the Ridgeway Community Church of the Brethren, Harrisburg, Pennsylvania, 15 April 1979.

[23]Robert W. Funk, *Jesus As Precursor* (Philadelphia: Fortress Press, 1975), p. 26.

[24]Kenneth L. Gibble, "Through the Looking Glass with Jesus," sermon delivered at the Ridgeway Community Church of the Brethren, Harrisburg, Pennsylvania, 1 March 1981.

[25]Van der Geest, p. 132.

[26]Ibid., p. 133.

[27]Fred B. Craddock, *As One Without Authority* (Enid, Oklahoma: Phillips University Press, 1974), p. 158.

[28]Jensen, p. 146.

[29]Ibid., p. 129.

[30]Flannery O'Connor, *Mystery and Manners* (New York: Farrar, Straus, and Giroux, 1969), p. 73.

[31]Kenneth L. Gibble, "The Wrath to Come," story/sermon delivered at the Ridgeway Community Church of the Brethren, Harrisburg, Pennsylvania, 29 August 1982.

[32]Niedenthal and Rice, "Preaching as Shared Story," in *Preaching the Story*, p. 3.

[33]Ann B. Ulanov, "The Psychological Reality of the Demonic," in *Disguises of the Demonic*, ed. Alan M. Olson (New York: Association Press, 1975), p. 144.

[34]Chaim Potok, *My Name Is Asher Lev* (New York: Alfred A. Knopf, 1972), p. 371.

Chapter V

[1]Eugene L. Lowry, *The Homiletical Plot: The Sermon as Narrative Art Form* (Atlanta: John Knox Press, 1980), p. 20.

[2]Frederick Buechner, in an interview with the author, 10 November 1982.

[3]Kenneth L. Gibble, "A God Who Terrifies," sermon delivered at the Ridgeway Community Church of the Brethren, Harrisburg, Pennsylvania, 7 November 1982.

[4]Frederick Buechner, *The Sacred Journey* (New York: Harper & Row, 1982), p. 6.

[5]Madeleine L'Engle, *The Irrational Season* (New York: Seabury Press, 1979), p. 17.

[6]Flannery O'Connor, *Mystery and Manners* (New York: Farrar, Straus and Giroux, 1969), p. 68.

[7]Amos N. Wilder, *Early Christian Rhetoric: The Language of the Gospel* (New York: Harper & Row, 1964), p. 65.

[8]On the subject of concrete language in funeral sermons, see my article, "In Memory of Martha," *The Christian Ministry*, January 1983.

[9]Fred B. Craddock, *As One Without Authority* (Enid, Oklahoma: Phillips University Press, 1974), p. 60.

[10]O'Connor, p. 91.

Chapter VI

[1]Walter Wink, *Transforming Bible Study* (Nashville: Abingdon, 1980), p. 102. In this same book, Wink also addresses the *limitations* of historical criticism.

[2]John A. Sanford, *Evil: the Shadow Side of Reality* (New York: Crossroad, 1981), p. 80.

[3]Bruce Vawter, *On Genesis: A New Reading* (New York: Doubleday & Company, Inc., 1977), p. 349.

[4]"The narrator, in what immediately follows, tells of a remarkable consequence which is related to the event of that night and therefore must be considered along with it." Gerhard von Rad, *Genesis: a Commentary*, rev. ed. (Philadelphia: The Westminster Press, 1972), p. 326.

[5]Vawter, p. 349.

[6]E. A. Speiser, *Genesis*, Anchor Bible, Vol. 1 (Garden City: Doubleday & Company, Inc., 1964), p. 253.

[7]Ibid., p. 255.

[8]von Rad, p. 319.

[9]Otto Eissfeldt, *The Old Testament: An Introduction* (New York: Harper & Row, 1965), p. 34.

[10]Jay A. Wilcoxen, "Narrative," in *Old Testament Form Criticism*, ed. John H. Hayes, Trinity University monograph series in religion, no. 2 (San Antonio: Trinity University Press, 1974), pp. 81–82.

[11]"We are dealing throughout with a tradition which was passed on by means of a very complicated process. It is not possible to recover the original setting and understanding of this narrative." Walter E. Rast, *Tradition History in the Old Testament* (Philadelphia: Fortress Press, 1972), p. 51.

[12]Robert Martin-Achard, "An Exegete Confronting Genesis 32:22–33," in *Structural Analysis and Biblical Exegesis*, ed. Dibran Y. Hadidian, Pittsburgh Theological Monograph Series, no. 3 (Pittsburgh: Pickwick Press, 1974), p. 41.

[13]" . . . it has been a common practice with many people to propitiate the fickle and dangerous spirits of the water at the fords." J. G. Frazer, *Folk-Lore in the Old Testament*, 3 vols. (London: Macmillan and Co., Ltd., 1919), 2:414.

[14]Ibid., p. 411.

[15]Theodore H. Gaster, *Myth, Legend, and Custom in the Old Testament* (New York: Harper & Row, 1969), p. 212.

[16]Ibid., pp. 206-7.

[17]Martin-Achard, p. 49.

[18]A. S. Herbert, *Genesis 12-50: Introduction and Commentary*, Torch Bible Commentaries (London: SCM Press Ltd., 1962), pp. 106-107.

[19]Nahum M. Sarna, *Understanding Genesis* (New York: Schocken Books, 1970), p. 206.

[20]See p. 4.

[21]Arthur I. Waskow, *Godwrestling* (New York: Schocken Books, 1978), pp. 1-2.

[22]Jerome Kodell, "Jacob Wrestles with Esau," *Biblical Theolcgy Bulletin* 10(April 1980):20.

[23]James Hillman, "Senex and Puer: An Aspect of the Historical and Psychological Present," *Eranos Jahrbuch* 36(1967):304.

[24]"The wound Jacob received is the mark a person carries who encounters spiritual reality as deeply as did Jacob. A person who has an experience of this psychological depth is always wounded by it." John A. Sanford, *The Man Who Wrestled With God: A Study of individuation (personal growth toward wholeness) based on four Bible stories* (King of Prussia: Religious Publishing Co., 1974), p. 46.

[25]Rollo May, *Love and Will* (New York: W. W. Norton, 1969), p. 171.

[26]"When belief is not yet shaken it already has the stories, and even after it is shaken by the most severe doubts we still have the stories." Stephen Crites, "Angels We Have Heard," in *Religion as Story*, ed. James B. Wiggins (New York: Harper & Row, 1975), p. 33.

[27]Amos N. Wilder, *Early Christian Rhetoric: The Language of the Gospel* (New York: Harper & Row, 1964), p. 126.

[28]James B. Wiggins, "Within and Without Stories," in *Religion as Story*, p. 20.

[29]Elie Wiesel, *The Gates of the Forest* (New York: Avon Books, 1967), p. 10.

[30]Elie Wiesel, *Messengers of God* (New York: Random House, Inc., 1976), pp. 124-125.

[31]Ibid., p. 132.

[32]Ibid., pp. xi-xiv.

[33]Waskow, p. 8.

[34]Ibid., p. 10.

[35]As an excellent introduction to the method of "telling" scripture, see Gary R. Vencil, "Storytelling and Interpretation: The Parable of the Widow and the Judge," *Explor* 5(Fall 1979):16–26.

[36]Waskow, p. 12.